The Best Seller!
The New Psychology of
Selling and Persuading People

The Best Seller!
The New Psychology of
Selling and Persuading People

RON WILLINGHAM

Prentice-Hall, Inc.
Englewood Cliffs, NJ

Prentice-Hall International, Inc., *London*
Prentice-Hall of Australia, Pty. Ltd., *Sydney*
Prentice-Hall of Canada Inc., *Toronto*
Prentice-Hall of India Private Ltd., *New Delhi*
Prentice-Hall of Japan, Inc., *Tokyo*
Prentice-Hall of Southeast Asia Pte. Ltd., *Singapore*
Whitehall Books, Ltd., *Wellington, New Zealand*
Editora Prentice-Hall do Brasil Ltda., *Rio de Janeiro*

© 1984 by

PRENTICE-HALL, INC.

Englewood Cliffs, NJ

Library of Congress Cataloging in Publication Data

Willingham, Ron
  The best seller!

  Includes index.
  1. Selling—Psychological aspects.   I. Title.
HF5438.8.P75W54   1984   658.8′5   83-19051
ISBN 0-13-071960-9
ISBN 0-13-074444-1 {PBK}

PRINTED IN THE UNITED STATES OF AMERICA

Foreword

Ron Willingham...

is a unique individual...destined to motivate multitudes in this and future generations to worthy achievements through his teaching and writing methods.

He has a strong religious faith and tries to apply it daily.

Ron has studied, learned, applied and taught the concepts of Positive Mental Attitude of other writers, teachers and lecturers...of the past as well as today.

He has designed and added his own unique methods, whereby he has often succeeded where others have failed.

The Best Seller is a book that will, no doubt, influence countless thousands of salespeople to reach higher goals and discover their better selves.

W. Clement Stone

Become Your Own Best Seller By Using This Book!

This book is about selling! You'll find it different from most you've ever read!

What's different about it?

Well, for starters, it puts the sales process into a simple six-step system. One that you can use—regardless of what you're selling.

People who've used my system say it's one of the most creative, dollar-producing sales aids they've ever discovered.

As I'm writing this, a marketing director for a world-wide company that I've conducted seminars for called me and told me that one of his salesmen closed a $250,000 sale by using my system. He also told of another salesman who reclaimed a very large corporate account that he'd previously lost.

I could go on and on!

I realize that these claims may sound like overkill and be hard for you to believe at this point. But you'll soon see what I mean.

You'll see how my system gives you an organized guide to follow—a track to run on, a competitive edge. It also shows you what to do, where to go next, and what went wrong when you didn't close.

Here are the six steps of the system:

1. Approach
2. Interview
3. Demonstrate
4. Validate

5. Negotiate

6. Close

You can fit whatever you're selling into this system—whether you're selling products, services, or ideas. All you have to do is add your own features, advantages, and benefits.

This system will teach you how to:

1. Gain rapport with people.

2. Identify their wants or needs.

3. Show how you can fill their wants or needs.

4. Prove that you can fill them.

5. Work out problems that keep them from buying.

6. Finalize the transaction.

I call this process, "Integrity Selling." It puts you in an interviewer or consultative role—a professional role. It's much more effective than old-fashioned sales methods. It's not uncommon for salespeople to increase their sales and earnings by 25 percent, 50 percent, or more by using my system! I realize that's promising you a lot. But you'll soon see that not only do I promise a lot, but more importantly—I deliver!

Another thing that makes this book different is that it helps you learn the psychology of persuasion. It'll help you learn techniques that very powerfully persuade people to like you, listen to you, trust you, believe you, and buy from you!

As you learn these techniques, your confidence will surge! You'll learn strategies for warming up cold customers, for neutralizing negative behavior of your prospects, and for dealing with stalls, put-offs, and objections.

I'll tell you how to develop your own success-support system. You'll see how being part of a support team will help plug you into a dynamo of power that's much greater than your own powers. As a result, you'll have more confidence. You'll think bigger. Your own personal belief system will expand.

My book will help you conquer an enemy that causes 90 percent of all salespeople to fail!

What is this enemy?

It's fear; fear of rejection, fear of poverty, and fear of the unknown. This enemy keeps us from making calls, from calling on the right people, or from asking people to buy.

In my book, I'll tell you about a super system that'll help you squeeze more dollars out of your time. One that'll also help you develop greater confidence in yourself.

You'll learn a mind-conditioning process that a very wealthy salesman once shared with me. He told me it was largely responsible for helping him earn several hundred-million dollars!

You'll discover how to get your customers selling themselves by using a method that exerts tremendous persuasion—without pressure from you. I'll share with you a strategy that helps you know when to close. One that actually conditions your prospects to give you affirmative responses.

You'll read an exciting strategy for dealing with price objections. You'll see that price objections usually aren't really price objections! You'll then be able to use them as powerful closing aids.

I'll share with you a new, unique formula for sales power. You'll see what causes success in selling. You'll learn strategies for doubling or tripling your sales power. I'll help you develop stronger trust relationships with your customers, which will give you an edge over your competition.

You'll find this short, easy-to-read book loaded with strategies and techniques that'll help you make more money! Ideas that are practical, workable, and result-producing.

Why have I earned the right to share these principles with you? That's a good question. You have a right to know.

I began selling when I was ten. I sold homeowners on paying me money to keep their lawns looking beautiful. I also sold a bowling-alley owner on paying me money to set up pins for his customers. Then I sold the customers on bowling in my lane. That was before the days of automatic pin-setting equipment. It was back-breaking work! I got paid

5 cents per line. But then, for only 15 cents I could buy a hamburger, a hot dog, and a Big Red soda pop for supper—all three!

In high school, I often had three jobs at the same time. I got up at 4:00 A.M. and loaded bread trucks. I delivered bread. I sold newspapers. I sold custom-made leather belts on which I hand-tooled people's names. I also paid my way through the first two years of college by making and selling these belts. That's been over thirty years ago, and I've been selling ever since.

Now, don't get the idea that I think I'm some Wonder Boy or Superstar! The truth is that I could write a thick book on *How to Waste Precious Time and Goof-Off While Supposedly Selling.* No one ever had greater call-reluctance or fear of rejection. I could write a book on that too, as well as on *How to Stretch Out Coffee Breaks and Kill Time Creatively!* So, you see, I had a long way to go! I had a lot to learn! I still do!

Since the early sixties, I've trained other people. I've written over twenty different training courses that have been conducted in forty states and several foreign countries and certified over 4,000 instructors to conduct them. At this point, over 100,000 people have gone through them.

I've listened to thousands of salespeople tell about their problems, fears, joys, and successes. I've seen many salespeople grow and become more successful. I've seen others bomb out and quit.

As a trainer and observer, I've analyzed many people's successes and failures—always asking, "Why?" Why do some succeed and why do some fail? This is what I've spent many years trying to figure out. What I've learned is what I'll write about in this book.

If someone had helped me learn thirty years ago what I'm sharing with you now, believe me, it would have meant a world of difference in my life, as well as in my own confidence level and income. I know from experience that if you'll practice the ideas that I'll give you, you'll earn several thousand times what this book cost you!

I'm excited about your getting this kind of return on your investment. So, for a moment, let me tell you how you can earn big baskets of green stuff as a result of reading this book!

The best way to get the most is to read it through as soon as you can—so you get a feel of what's in it. Then, come back to the first chapter and carefully read it again. Underline ideas. Write in the margin. Make notes. As you read, ask yourself, "What does this mean to me, and how can I apply what I've just read?" Jot down your responses. Commit yourself to take action!

Do this each day for a week on the first chapter. Then go to the next one. Spend a whole week on it. Scan it several times that week. Practice the action guides. Make mental and written notes on the results you get. Then, go through the other chapters in the same way.

Why do I suggest this slow, plodding, repetitious method? Because, in order to make money for you, these ideas must be engrained in your subconscious as *habits*, grooved so deeply that you practice them *instinctively*, and they become *automatic* responses!

I've found that not many people understand this or are willing to put up with the repetition that this involves. So they rob themselves of the rewards they'd otherwise enjoy. To fix these skill levels in your automatic-habit responses, it takes practice, practice, practice; such practice as it would take to become a skilled surgeon or an all-pro linebacker, or a scratch golfer. The key words are: action, study, examination, and more action!

Well, since this is an action book, and you bought it with the hopes of increasing your income, let's quit all this talking. Let's taxi down for a take-off, open wide our throttles, and thunder down the runway!

We'll soar into chapter 1, which will give you some strategies for increasing your sales power and income. Then, once we've gained altitude, we'll blast into chapter 2. In it, we'll begin with the first step of my sales system.

The System

Here's my six-step system of selling that you'll learn in this book. Look it over and study it for a few minutes. You'll notice that each step has four action guides to practice. Now, don't let all these guides swamp you when you first read them. Don't feel as though you could never do all these things. The purpose of this book is to teach you, gradually, to practice them.

Here's the system:

Approach

1. Tune the world out and your prospects in.
2. Put them at ease and make them feel important.
3. Get them talking about themselves.
4. Hold eye contact and listen to how they feel.

Interview

1. Ask open-ended, indirect questions that draw out wants or needs.
2. Listen to and paraphrase all points—write them down.
3. Identify dominant wants or needs—get their agreement.
4. Assure them that you want to help them select the right product.

Demonstrate

1. Repeat their dominant wants or needs.
2. Demonstrate the product or service that will answer them.
3. Avoid talking about price—make it secondary to finding out what best fills their needs.
4. Ask for their reactions, feelings, or opinions.

Validate

1. Translate product features into customer benefits.
2. Justify price and emphasize value.

3. Offer proof-of-benefit and satisfied users.
4. Reassure and reinforce prospects to neutralize fear of buying.

Negotiate

1. Ask, "Is there anything that's keeping you from buying now?"
2. Welcome objections—let prospects know that you understand how they feel.
3. Identify specific objections—get agreement that these are the only ones.
4. Discuss possible solutions—ask prospects' opinions for best solutions.

Close

1. Ask trial-closing questions to get opinions and response.
2. Give positive reinforcement.
3. Restate how benefits will outweigh costs.
4. Ask them to buy now—hold eye contact and silently wait for their answer.

In this book, you'll take each step as a bite-sized chunk and chew it until it's digested. Then, you'll go to the next step.

To help you remember these six steps, memorize this acronym: *AID, Inc.*

AID, Inc. stands for Approach, Interview, Demonstrate, Val-I-Date (rather than "validate"), Negotiate, Close. Say this now. Say it a couple of dozen times, and you'll have it memorized.

Ron Willingham

Contents

CONTENTS

Chapter One

Ron Willingham's Secret Formula For Tripling Your Sales Power!

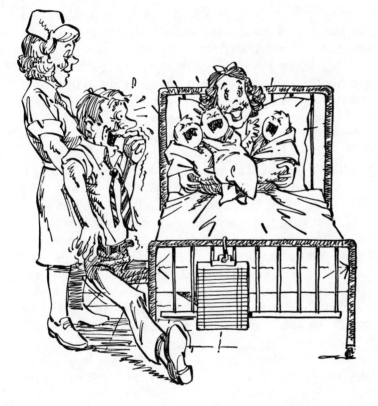

L ouis Hartzog is one of the most successful roofing salesmen in his part of Alabama.

Does he possess a magic potion that makes him a super salesman? Hardly! He's quiet and unassuming.

Does he possess the courage of a Richard the Lion-hearted, able to overwhelm homeowners? No! In fact he admits to a very high degree of call-reluctance—fear of rejection.

Does he possess the fast-thinking, dazzling brilliance of a flashy superstar? Not at all! According to him, he's "just an ole' country boy who's pulled himself up by his bootstraps!"

So then, what is it about Louis that causes him to excel in his field of selling? Maybe this example will give you an answer.

Louis says that he's always had a very high degree of call-reluctance, but, because of his high desire to succeed, he's found a way to deal with it.

When he drives up in front of a prospect's home, he gets out of his car and walks around looking at his tires as if suspecting one of them to be low in air. He selects the rear tire opposite the person's home, inspects it, and then kicks it several times. As he kicks it, supposedly to see if it needs more air, he gives himself a pep talk. He says "O.K., Louis Hartzog, you're nervous about going up to this person's home. But you know what you're sellin'. You're honest and want to do a good job. These people can rely on you. So—get on up there and ring the doorbell, and act confident!"

After saying this, Louis bounces up to the door and rings the bell—standing a super chance of making the sale.

Now... stop a moment and think about this real story. What is it about Louis Hartzog that causes him to be successful in selling? What's one of the keys to his high sales achievement? As you think about this question, let me ask you a couple more: Why are some salespeople successful— and others aren't? Why do some salespeople enjoy a luxurious lifestyle; some just barely get by; and others bomb out? Why? What's the real cause of success in selling?

First, let me tell you what it *isn't*. It's not brains! Some of the most intelligent people I know couldn't sell a life raft to a drowning sailor! It's not good looks or appearance! I've conducted seminars for salespeople in which the sharpest-looking person was the weakest sales performer!

It's not product knowledge! Usually the people who know the most about a product or service are the ones back at the home office who pore over their calculators, charts, and tables all day. They may have tremendous knowledge but be unable to relate to ordinary people. Some of them couldn't sell if you held a gun to their heads.

Well, if success in selling isn't because of brains, sharp appearance, or product knowledge, then to what is it due? What's the real reason why some salespeople feast on filet mignon; others settle for salami sandwiches; and still others are content with crumbs?

WHAT SEPARATES THE WINNERS FROM THE LOSERS?

Well, in the event that I've aroused your curiosity, I'm going to share with you what the success factor in selling is. Not only will I share it with you, I'll also tell you how you can increase it within yourself!

But first, let me say that successful salespeople come in all sizes and shapes. There are short ones, tall ones, young ones, old ones, introverts, extroverts.

They don't fit molds. They aren't stamped out like cookies from an assembly line. They don't ride a constant-lucky streak, nor do they possess special secrets or magic powers.

Some look sharp and professional. Others don't stand out in a crowd. Some have the gift of gab. Others are quiet and even shy. Some drive Cadillacs and flash diamond rings. Others drive Volkswagens and quietly bank their money.

But all successful salespeople share a common trait!

ALL SUCCESSFUL SALESPEOPLE SHARE A COMMON TRAIT!

This one universal characteristic not only accounts for success in selling, but it also *multiplies* sales power. It can do the same for you! It can when you really learn about it—and then when you do it!

What is this common success factor in selling, and what is the secret factor that could triple your sales power? Well, in order to explain it, let me share with you this formula. I call it the Formula for Sales Power. This formula explains why some salespeople do better than others—why some fail and others succeed. It also explains the elements that go together to make up sales power. When I refer to "sales power," I refer to the net result, the bottom line, the amount for which we close and get paid. What we make happen!

A FORMULA FOR SALES POWER

Here's the formula:

Product Knowledge,	*plus*
Sales Know-How,	*plus*
Persuasive Ability,	*times*
Achievement Drive,	*equal*
Sales Power!	

Now before you read on, stop a moment or so and run this formula through your computer again. As you do so, you will quickly pick out the common ingredient that all successful salespeople have; the one thing that, more than anything else, guarantees success in selling.

Yes, see if you can isolate the success factor in selling! It's the main trait that successful salespeople have in common.

As you're thinking, let's take a moment or so and talk about this formula.

PRODUCT KNOWLEDGE

Product knowledge is how well you know your product or service. It's the technical information that you must know in order to present what you're selling as well as answer questions that you're asked.

It's been estimated that over 90 percent of sales training is in product knowledge. Many, many sales managers think that if their salespeople know their product or service well, they can sell it. Few things could be farther from the truth!

Don't get me wrong. Product knowledge is very important and necessary! But having it doesn't guarantee success in selling!

SALES KNOW-HOW

Sales know-how evolves from experience. It only comes after you've had game experience. It's ring-savvy, street smarts. It's knowing what to say, and when, and how in order to make a sale. It's the result of trial and error, trial and success. Only because of experience can you develop the know-how of what to do in certain situations. You don't develop sales know-how in a classroom, or from a book, or from a sales course. It's gained only by experience!

While this is true, I also need to say that you can have a lot of sales experience and very little know-how. You can because you didn't choose to *learn* from your experience.

You learn from your sales experiences when you constantly review your performance; when you reflect, question, and grade yourself at the end of each call or each day's calls.

So, remember—sales experience doesn't guarantee sales know-how, but *learning* from experience does!

PERSUASIVE ABILITY

The third element of the Sales-Power Formula is persuasive ability, which is the skill or finesse with which you're able to develop rapport and trust with people. This is necessary before you can have a successful, convincing sales communication.

Persuasive ability is how effective you are in transferring your own conviction and enthusiasm to others.

It's true that some people seem to have a natural gift or talent for persuading people. While this is true, I think that any of us can strengthen or develop our persuasive powers significantly. Any of us can, starting where we are, build more effective persuasive skills.

It's been my experience, unfortunately, that most sales-people get almost no training in interpersonal communications.

And since they get very little training in this area, most have entirely the wrong concept of what's involved in persuasion!

Many think that it's talking, telling, convincing.

It isn't that at all!

What is it?

Well, I believe that persuasion is done best through interaction—by asking questions, soliciting opinions, actively listening and giving feedback, and by putting yourself in the prospect's shoes.

Persuasion operates on a much more in-depth, emotional level, too, through empathy, by giving psychological value, and by listening to how another person feels!

Incidentally, we'll talk about all these factors in this book.

ACHIEVEMENT DRIVE

In this fourth part of the Sales-Power Formula lies the secret of success and achievement in selling. In it we see the one common ingredient that all successful salespeople have. This fact has been validated in research experiments as well as on the streets and in office buildings where salespeople win and lose.

Dr. David C. McClellan of Harvard University has devoted much of his life to the study of achievement drive. His studies prove conclusively what thousands of others have observed from practical experience—that achievement drive is the *multiplier* of all your other skills and abilities. It's the multiplier! By this I mean that when you add your product knowledge, sales know-how, and persuasive ability, you then multiply them by your achievement drive to arrive at your sales power.

That's heavy stuff!

YOUR ACHIEVEMENT DRIVE MULTIPLIES ALL YOUR OTHER SKILLS AND ABILITIES!

Let me explain it this way. Suppose that on a scale of 1 to 10 your product knowledge is a 7, your sales know-how is 8, and your persuasive ability is 7. Add these three sums and you get 22. Now, let's suppose that your *achievement drive,* or *desire,* or *will-to-sell* is pretty low. Let's say it's a 3. Since your achievement drive is the *multiplier,* you multiply 3 by 22 to arrive at your sales power. In this case it's 66.

Now, to demonstrate how achievement drive multiplies your other abilities and skills, suppose that it's 9 instead of 3. Then to arrive at your sales power, you'd multiply 9 by 22. In this case your sales power is 198. Or three times what it was before!

Does this jangle your juices just to think about it? Does it help you better understand the success factor in selling? I hope so. Because it reveals to us not only the common ingredient that successful salespeople have, but also a method by which we can all increase our sales power. We increase our sales power by increasing our *will-to-sell,* our *desire,* our *achievement drive!*

HOW TO INCREASE ACHIEVEMENT DRIVE

"O.K.," you say, "I understand the importance of high desire; that it's the multiplier; and that it increases my sales power. But *how* do I go about developing more of it?"

Good! I'm glad you asked!

Dr. McClellan, to whose studies on achievement drive I referred earlier, explains that *everyone* has achievement drive, but not everyone has learned how to *release* it! You see, achievement drive is already in us waiting to be released. It's not something that we pour in. It's something that we let out!

To me this is a very important distinction. Achievement drive is released from within; it's not injected from without!

You increase your achievement drive by releasing what's already there. You can release it in these ways:

1. By setting realistic, believable goals.
2. By dwelling on the rewards of reaching those goals.
3. By associating with high achievers.
4. By developing and nurturing success-support systems.
5. By building strong belief in what you're selling.
6. By viewing yourself as a value generator.

Your present level of achievement drive has much to do with your self-esteem, with your background, and with the level of past successes you've experienced. It's largely controlled by your own personal belief-system.

ALL SALESPEOPLE OPERATE WITHIN THEIR "AREA OF THE POSSIBLE"!

Your mental paradigm—the way you view yourself, your world, and the relationship that both have together—governs your "area of the possible"! All your actions, feelings, behavior, and abilities are consistent with your "area of the possible"! Pardon me for playing Socrates with you, but this last sentence is worthy of re-reading and pondering a few dozen times!

Incidentally, much of this book's content is designed to help you increase and enlarge your own mental paradigm—your "area of the possible"—your personal belief-system. That's why it's so important that you view this book as a system of guides that you apply and practice rather than as merely information that you learn!

Why? Because your belief system, or self-esteem, is changed only by experiencing! It's not changed by intellectually knowing!

But, back to our thoughts on achievement drive.

HOW IS ACHIEVEMENT DRIVE REVEALED?

Achievement drive is revealed in you by such things as: energy, enthusiasm, being hungry for knowledge and information, ambition, aggressiveness, persistence, creativity, time consciousness, and being bottom-line oriented.

Woven throughout this book are strategies to help you release more achievement drive. As you successfully employ these strategies, your sales power will be multiplied.

In salespeople, high achievement drive is demonstrated by these work habits:

1. Making as many calls as possible on good prospects
2. Planning each call—having a specific objective to accomplish
3. Asking the prospect to buy

The main reasons why most salespeople fail are: they simply don't make enough calls on good prospects; they don't have a planned agenda for each call; they don't ask the prospect to buy! They don't do these things because they lack the inner drive, or motivation, to overcome inertia, fear of rejection, and weak selling skills.

SET MOTIVATIONAL GOALS

One of the secrets of high-performance selling, or releasing achievement drive, is in setting motivational goals. A motivational goal is something you want to have, do, become, or enjoy. The trick is to set motivational goals that you'll give yourself as rewards for reaching your sales goals. A motivational goal motivates us to go out and sell in order to earn enough money or recognition to get the things we want.

Most of us aren't really motivated by money alone. We're motivated by things that money will allow us to have. New homes, automobiles, clothes, investments, recognition, trips—these are a few of the things that give us reasons to work to earn money.

Some years ago I worked as a consultant for a rather colorful man, W. Clement Stone. Mr. Stone had started with $100 and built a company that had a net profit that year of $100 million.

One day I was visiting with Mike Ritt, who'd been with the company over thirty years. I asked him, "How was Mr. Stone able to build a company this size?"

He took a moment to think and then said, "Well, he's one smart man! And...he knows how to motivate salesmen.

"I remember the old days when he worked more directly with the salesmen and sales managers. He'd get the people to go to the bank and borrow money to buy our stock. He'd take a guy into an automobile showroom and get him all excited about buying a new car.

"What he'd do was get the person in debt—so he'd have to work like crazy to pay it off. That meant he'd have to go out and sell more insurance in order to come up with the money. He kept 'em motivated," Mike emphasized.

"His theory was that if a man is honest, he'll pay his debts. And when an honest man is in debt, he'll work hard to get out! He knows how to get the most out of a person!" he concluded.

TAKE ACTION NOW TO INCREASE YOUR MOTIVATION

Now, while you're thinking about the power of setting motivational goals to release achievement drive within yourself, why not stop and do something about it? Right now, will you stop and think of something you'd really enjoy having, something that you wouldn't ordinarily go out and buy. Maybe it's a luxury item. Maybe it's something you'd feel a bit extravagant in buying. It might be a new car, a new wardrobe, new golf clubs, a new briefcase, a trip to Hawaii or Europe—anything that really excites you.

Make it a fairly short-range goal. If you've not done this before, you'll want to set motivational goals that you can reach in a month or so. The reason is that you'll feel more pressure to achieve them, and you'll also enjoy an earlier victory.

First, select the thing you want to have—the reward that you'll present to yourself when you reach a specific sales goal.

Write it down; get a picture of it in your mind. Get a real picture of it to look at each day.

Then select the sales-volume goal that you'll have to reach before you reward yourself with the motivational goal.

Write it down also. In fact, write out this statement on an index card: "By July 30, I'll sell $500,000 of life insurance (or whatever you want to sell)."

Then continue by writing, "When I reach this goal, I'll reward myself by buying a new briefcase (or whatever you most want)."

Analyze this and you'll see that you have set a:

1. Sales-volume goal

2. Target date

3. Motivational goal

I can assure you that if the motivational goal is something you really want, it'll be a strong power in helping you reach your sales goal. Your mental computer, that mind within you, will be fueled by strong emotional desire. It'll work night and day for you—helping you figure out the most efficient ways to reach your sales-volume goal.

Robert Hooten was in a training course I conducted years ago. He'd just bought a small printing firm. He was broke, had little cash flow, and had creditors hounding him. After I challenged the class to set motivational goals, he decided he would. He set a goal to get a Jaguar sportscar. The condition was that he'd have to be doing at least $40,000 monthly volume in his shop and have the cash to pay for it. It seemed impossible!

But he cut out a picture of the model he wanted: a white one with a dark-cloth top and biscuit-leather seats. He tacked the picture on his office wall. Everyday he looked at it, and looked at it, and looked at it—visualizing himself already owning it. It became a passion with him. So much so that it kept him going—through extremely difficult times, when it looked as if his world would cave in on him.

Then one day he came into my office, pitched a set of car keys on my desk, and said, "Come outside and see 'our' car!" Taking me outside, he proudly pointed at a new Jaguar sportscar parked at the curb—identical in every detail to the picture he'd hung up a few years back!

SUGGESTIONS THAT'LL HELP YOU RELEASE MORE ACHIEVEMENT DRIVE

Here are some other suggestions that'll help you release achievement drive. Cut out pictures of your motivational goal, then put them around, so you see them several times each day.

Go window-shopping. Go to dealer's showrooms, department stores, travel agencies—wherever you'll see your desired goal. Look at it. Feel it. Touch it, taste it, hold it, ride it—get used to being around it. Do this window-shopping as often as you can.

Then, when you reach your sales-volume goal, immediately go out and get the motivational goal. Present it to yourself! Now, promise me that you won't cheat! Don't reach your sales goal and then chicken out of rewarding yourself. If you're like me, you may have second thoughts and feel extravagant in rewarding yourself. But, remember—a deal's a deal! So pay yourself.

SUMMING UP

Let's take a moment and review this first chapter. First, I suggested a Formula for Sales Power, which will help you analyze your sales power. It also suggests a method of increasing your sales effectiveness. The formula is:

Product Knowledge, *plus*
Sales Know-How, *plus*

Persuasive Ability,   *times*
Achievement Drive,   *equal*
Sales Power

How do you honestly rate yourself on this scale? On a scale of 1 to 10, how do you rate in each area? Then, what is your total sales-power rating?

Now you see that achievement drive is the *multiplier* of your other skills and abilities. How much effort will you spend following the suggestions I outlined for releasing more of your will-to-sell? Will you actually stop and take time to set your own motivational goals? Please do so before you go to the next chapter. Will you do it and not just think about it? Don't just think about it, do it! This is the only way you'll benefit!

After you've written your sales-volume goal, target date, and motivational goal, then attack the next chapter. It's entitled, "APPROACH-How to Get People to Unlock Their Mental Gates and Let You In!"

In it you'll learn the first step in my system of selling. Specifically, you'll learn and practice some strategies that'll increase your skill in approaching people.

Use the strategies, and people will open up to you more easily. They'll unfold their arms quicker. The ice will melt faster.

You'll also develop more confidence as you call on people. You'll learn how to set the stage for more effective communications and persuasion.

Come back and re-read this first chapter. Re-read and re-read. Look for the essence of truth that it contains. If you're really looking, keep on searching until you find it, and then apply what you discover. This chapter can give you the secret for tripling your sales power!

Willingham's Wisdom

There was once a ragged salesperson named Stowe,
Whose achievement drive was pathetically low!
    But when a motivational goal he set,
    Caused him to work until his other goals were met,
It wasn't long until he was rolling in the dough!

                             (Like this model, Aristotle?)

Chapter Two

APPROACH—
How to Get People to Unlock Their Mental Gates and Let You In!

It's been over twenty years now. Although I'd never met him before, and haven't seen him since, I still clearly remember his name.

It was Jack Lopez Klein.

One day, Jack Lopez Klein came into my furniture store, introduced himself, and made quite an impression on me.

"Ron," he said, "my name is Jack Lopez Klein. My name is very important to me, and I'd like for you to remember it!"

His mannerisms immediately attracted my attention. He was quiet but seemed very confident. He looked directly into my eyes as he spoke. I was impressed by his sincerity.

"You can remember my name," he went on, "if you'll remember these things."

He looked at me—I had a feeling that he was checking me out to make sure I was listening.

" 'Jack' is American, and I'm proud to be an American. 'Lopez' is Spanish, and I was born in Mexico. 'Klein' is Jewish, and I'm Jewish."

Wow! How could I ever forget an introduction like that?

We sat down and continued visiting. He was much shorter than I was. He wore cowboy boots. His hair was thin to balding. His nose seemed to zigzag all over his face. He had a malformed upper lip.

Clark Gable he wasn't! But a super, genuine, professional salesperson he was!

After we chatted for a few minutes, he told me what furniture manufacturers he represented and said, "I see by looking around your store that my lines wouldn't fit in with the styles you carry."

"Really," he went on, "I knew that anyway, but I just wanted to come in and meet you."

He visited for a while, had some nice things to say about my store, and, in a short time, he was gone. And as I mentioned, I've never seen him since.

Not long after that I noticed in a trade journal that he'd been voted the outstanding wholesale-furniture salesman in the Southwest.

I wasn't surprised.

I've thought about Jack Lopez Klein many times since then—remembering the impact his approach had on me. I can still recall sitting and talking to him, wanting to buy something from him because his approach impressed me so much.

In my system of selling, the first step is the *approach*. The purpose of the approach step is to gain rapport with prospects, to break the ice, to get them to mentally unfold their arms—to listen to you without bias, preconceived ideas, or prejudices. To break down their preoccupation barriers. To allow you into their space.

THE APPROACH STEP PREPARES YOUR PROSPECTS TO LISTEN!

The approach step prepares your prospects to listen to what you have to say.

Think for a moment. Whenever a salesperson approaches you—what runs through your mind? Does your guard automatically go up?

Here are some typical tapes we all play: "What does this person want with me?" "Why am I wasting my time with him or her?" As the encounter progresses, we play other tapes: "I'll be nice to him or her, cut 'em off as soon as I can, and then get back to work." Or we've all played this tape: "I've got to get this report out in one hour! It's a three-hour job! And this turkey is taking up my time!"

You get the idea.

My point is that you can't get to first base with prospects until you've gained rapport, or comfortable relations, with them; until you've gotten their attention. This step should be the first goal or objective in your sales calls—whether the calls are made in person or on the telephone; whether you're calling on old, repeat customers or on someone for the first time.

DON'T PROCEED WITH THE SALE UNTIL YOU'VE GAINED RAPPORT!

I'll repeat this at the end of this chapter, but let me also say that you usually waste your time when you try to proceed with the sale—if you don't first successfully develop rapport. This is important to remember because most prospects are preconditioned to put on the brakes whenever a salesperson approaches.

If you don't believe this, go by for a friendly visit with your banker. Tell him you were close by the bank, had only a couple of minutes, but just wanted to say "Hi."

Then ask him about his family, or where he's going on vacation, or about the upcoming football game.

Watch his body language. He'll probably lean back in his chair, relax, and occasionally even smile! (Yes, even bankers have been known to smile at times!)

Contrast this with the next time you go in to ask for a loan. You'll think he's two different people. His guard goes up. He gets a strange glaze in his eyes and begins asking a whole bunch of rather suspicious questions.

You might remember this slightly exaggerated example to make a point. The point is that people are different when we're trying to sell them something from when we're there for social reasons.

Incidentally, while we're on the subject, did you hear the one about the businessman who was really down on his luck? High-interest rates were killing him. His costs had skyrocketed. His cash flow had stopped flowing. His notes were due at the bank, and so in desperation he went in, got on his hands and knees, and begged the banker to extend his notes.

"No," the banker shot back. "We can no longer extend them!"

"But I can't pay," the businessman pleaded.

"Then we'll foreclose and take all your assets," the banker replied with cool dispassion.

"Please," the man pleaded.

Finally, the banker softened slightly, thought, and said, "Well, maybe I will give you a chance."

Clearing his throat, he went on, "No one has ever known it, but one of my eyes is a glass eye. It's such a perfect match that my wife can't even tell the difference.

"Tell you what I'll do. If you can tell me which eye is the glass eye, I'll extend your notes for 120 days."

Delighted, the businessman relaxed, breathed a sigh of relief, smiled confidently, and pointed, "It's the left one!"

"Incredible!" responded the banker. "That's incredible!" "How in the world did you know?"

"Oh, I knew immediately, " the businessman answered, "the left one is the one with a glimmer of compassion in it!"

Now that I've told this story, I hope I can get my notes paid off before this book comes out.

Let's get back to our subject of gaining rapport with prospects.

UNTIL PROSPECTS WANT TO LISTEN TO YOU, THEY WON'T!

The truth is that unless a person *wants* to listen to you, and *wants* to hear you, and *wants* to trust you; you'll constantly run into brick walls.

A few years ago I was doing training seminars for federally funded local agencies. In the seminars, unemployed people were trained to get jobs.

One of my staff people made an appointment for me to personally call on Billy Don Everett, whose office was 500 miles from my home. I flew into Austin, Texas, rented a car, and drove up to Belton for a 3:30 P.M. appointment with Billy Don. Hoping to see him, I arrived 45 minutes early. He wasn't in. When 3:30 came, he still wasn't in. Finally, he sauntered in at 4:15. Looking as though he could still play linebacker on most any team, he looked at me and said, "Are you still here?"

"Well, uh, yeah," I replied, tugging at the inside of my collar.

"Well, you're wasting your time," he shot back.

"I am?"

"Yeah, I told that boy who called me that I wasn't interested in your training. You're just wasting your time!"

"What did he say when you told him that?" I asked, smiling (as much as I could).

"He asked me to wait and make that decision *after* you'd talked to me."

Then he went on, "Well, I guess as long as you're here you might as well tell me what you've got. How much is it?"

Ducking his question, I explained that I had set up and was ready to run a videotape of a seminar we'd done for an agency similar to his.

"Well, turn it on," he motioned, with about as much enthusiasm as an old mother cow chewing her cud.

I flipped it on. It was a twenty-minute tape. About halfway through it, he got up and walked out! Without saying a word, he just walked out and left me with two of his staff people.

When the film finished, I nervously made small talk with them. Finally, in ten to fifteen minutes, he wandered back into the room.

"You still here?" he asked.

By this time I was ready to kill him—which he sensed. And sensing it gave him all kinds of pleasure. He turned a chair backwards and sat down. Resting his forearms on the chairback, he grinned at me.

"O.K., sell me!" he said.

I felt a great deal in common with General Custer! Quickly I realized that I had indeed wasted my time and money, and since this was the case, a little gamble couldn't hurt anything.

So I pulled my chair up close to him, looked squarely into his right eyeball, and said, "Billy Don, Willie Taylor (a friend of his) told me that you run the *worst* office in the whole state!" Saying that, I shut up and looked at him! And in a moment he just died laughing! He roared!

Then he said, "Did he really say that?"

"No, he really didn't," I said. "He said that you run a very efficient office. He also said that you'd give me a line of bull ten-feet deep!"

He grinned as if I'd paid him the highest compliment possible. He relaxed. We talked. I found out that his high-school football coach is a friend of mine. After a couple of hours, which ran much later than office hours, we tentatively agreed on the details for a seminar I'd do for his people.

As I was leaving, he apologized for the treatment he'd given me and bestowed the greatest honor on me that any genuine Texas redneck could bestow. He said, "I'll tell you one thing, I'd sure as hell hate to get into a poker game with you!"

I grinned at him and said, "Billy Don, you'd win everytime!"

He liked that!

We became good friends.

My point, of course, is that I'd never have gotten close to making a sale if I hadn't gained rapport with him. Admittedly, it was a bit unusual, but we developed a good relationship.

ACTION GUIDES TO HELP YOU GAIN RAPPORT!

Let me mention four action guides you can take that will help you establish rapport with your prospects. These are actions you can practice this week as you approach people. The four action guides are:

1. Tune the world out and your prospects in.
2. Put them at ease and make them feel important.
3. Get them talking about themselves.
4. Hold eye contact and listen to how they feel.

Doing these four actions will help you get your prospects to drop their defenses and listen to you. The guides employ strong, effective, psychological, and human-relations principles.

TUNE THE WORLD OUT AND YOUR PROSPECTS IN

You can best do this by putting your full attention on your prospects and what's in their environment. Environments can tell you a great deal about people if you'll listen with your eyes.

For several years, I was so self-conscious in calling on people that I didn't really notice things about them. Until I learned to control it, fear kept me from noticing clues about establishing rapport.

Few people in the world, if any, are like Billy Don Everett. He gave me all kinds of clues as to how he'd like me to relate to him. All I had to do was listen with my eyes, ears, and intuitions.

Early in my selling life, I was so intent on trying to make a good impression on my prospects that I didn't program any feedback from them.

Since I'm a very sensitive person, I've always cared how people feel about me. This caused me to be much too self-centered—to think too much of how I was impressing my prospects, instead of how they were impressing me.

Very often tenseness and stage fright choke off our ability to relax ourselves...as well as our prospects. These emotions blind us to obvious clues that lie around in our prospects' environments.

The secret is to re-direct our focus; to get our awareness off ourselves and on our prospects; to notice their mannerisms, their gestures, their clothes, their enviroment, as well as the way they sit, talk, look at us, use their hands, etc.

Consciously focusing on your prospects and their environment helps you tune the world out and them in. It also helps you forget your own nervousness—it gets your mind off yourself and on your prospects. And, it's something anyone can develop the habit of doing.

PUT THEM AT EASE AND MAKE THEM FEEL IMPORTANT!

The second action guide is to put your prospects at ease and make them feel important. You can best do this by appearing to be at ease yourself. It depends on the environment and the person, of course, but generally a friendly, relaxed way of approaching someone is best.

People do mirror your actions. For most people, there's a subconscious urge to adopt the same emotional level that you present to them. There are exceptions, of course, but you have to go with percentages. And, I'm convinced that most prospects are influenced by your behavior mode.

Usually the worst thing you can do is go in and immediately make a sales presentation. This scene usually sets up resistances that block you. You should always carefully establish rapport *before* you get into your selling, telling, and demonstrating.

Also, it's best to leave your briefcase closed and not to pull out your sales material right away. It's usually best not to give your prospects the feeling that you're trying to "put something over on them."

In gaining rapport, be aware that your body language influences your prospects. Watch how and where you sit. Don't get too close or crowd your prospects' space. Don't get too familiar or casual or too stiff and formal, either.

Lean back and show open gestures. Don't lean in too far. Don't sit so close that your prospects feel uncomfortable. Watch where they have their guests' chairs located in relation to their desks. This tips off where they want you.

If your prospect is right-handed, sit or stand just to his or her right-of-center. When you're standing, don't get closer than arm's length to your prospect. Always try to sense quickly where he or she wants you to be—where he or she's most comfortable having you.

You can make people feel important by, first of all, *thinking* they're important. If you can do it sincerely, compliment them on things others have said about them or things you like in their surroundings. Laugh and smile to break the tension.

These actions and feelings are very powerful in helping your prospects feel at ease with you. They seem to work best when you do them naturally. Natural responses are developed by conscious, repetitive practice.

GET THEM TALKING ABOUT THEMSELVES

The third action guide is "Get Them Talking About Themselves." You can do this by asking nonthreatening questions about things in your prospect's environment.

People love to talk about their own interests. They're not threatened by this type of conversation.

I called on a man recently. In gathering information about him, someone told me that he fancied himself as somewhat of a big-league hunter.

Sure enough when I got into his office, there was a beautiful stuffed pheasant on his credenza. There were paintings of ducks and other waterfowl on his walls.

You know the rest of the story.

He didn't buy an idea I presented—it really didn't fit his needs. But it surely was easy to establish quick rapport with him.

Most people love to tell us what they do in their spare time. They love to talk about their families.

"How did you get into this line of work?" "How long have you been with this company?" "Where have you previously lived?" "What led you to come with this firm?" These are easy questions that get people talking.

"How many people work under you?" is a question that gets interesting responses. First of all, it says that you recognize the person as one in authority. It also gives her or him a chance to turn the question into a joke or humorous response with a response such as, "Oh, about half of them!" Then your laughing together helps break the tension.

"How did you get into your line of work?" is an excellent question to constantly have ready to use.

"What contributed most to helping you get where you are now?" is another effective question to ask almost anyone.

These and other nonthreatening questions help draw out your prospects. They're natural ones to get them talking, you listening, and both of you relaxing.

How much time you spend with these approach questions depends upon the prospect and the nature of your visit. If you're selling a high-ticket item or service, you'll probably need to spend more time. If you sense that your prospect wants to get on with things, then move on.

HOLD EYE CONTACT AND LISTEN TO HOW THEY FEEL

The fourth action guide that'll help you develop rapport with your prospects is to hold eye contact and listen to how they *feel!*

I've developed the habit of focusing both of my eyes on just one of my prospects' eyes. I believe this does two things: first, it causes me to make a stronger impact upon them; and, second, it plugs me into them so I can better receive their feelings and emotions. This allows me to listen to their words as well as to their emotions.

You may want to try this same thing. This concentrated eye contact may seem a bit weird at first, but if you'll do it for twenty-one days, it'll become a habit.

Professional communicators, such as salespeople, counselors, and teachers, know the value of listening for feelings and not just for words. There's a word for this. It's *empathy!* When you have empathy, you feel with another person—you take on that person's feelings, perceptions, and emotions.

Listening for feelings puts you on a deeper-than-average communication level. When prospects sense that you care how they feel, they'll more quickly drop their defenses and let you into their space. Practicing this action guide powerfully impacts upon your selling! It helps you develop quick rapport.

GIVE YOUR PROSPECTS PLENTY OF FEEDBACK

Your prospects will sense that you care how they feel when: first, you really do care; and second, you give them feedback that *proves* you care. What kind of feedback? Well, you can do such things as nodding approval and leaning forward to catch important things they say, and giving verbal responses such as, "I see," "Yes, I agree," "I understand how you feel," or "I see what you mean." These forms of feedback are very powerful and let your prospects know that you understand how they feel.

In the process of persuasion, which is what a sale is, it's just as important to give feedback to people as it is to listen to them. Think for a moment and see if the people you communicate best with don't give you plenty of feedback. Also, the people you communicate worst with probably give you little feedback.

I hate to talk to someone who just sits there like a fireplug and gives me no feedback. It makes me feel very uncomfortable.

Your prospects also feel uncomfortable when you don't give them feedback as they talk.

YOU APPROACH DIFFERENT PEOPLE IN DIFFERENT WAYS!

As we near the end of this chapter, let me say that you approach different people in different ways. All people are different, and you communicate with them differently.

Some are social and love to talk about people and things. Others are administrative types and want to keep everything businesslike. Others are creative and want to talk about ideas and concepts. Others want to talk about end-results and are very time-conscious.

The secret is to feel intuitively how different individuals want you to relate to them. How can you do this? Well, everyone leaves clues that tell how he or she wants you to relate. The clues are in a person's actions and environment.

Part of your professionalism depends upon how well you pick up and process these clues.

SUMMING UP

Remember the main point of this chapter: you must gain rapport with your prospects *before* you can sell, tell, or demonstrate to them.

You can enhance your ability to gain rapport with a person by practicing the four action guides that I've just discussed.

This approach step is the first step in my system of selling. The best way to make these action guides your own is to consciously practice them each day for a week.

Scan this chapter several times this week. You'll find that practicing these action guides will cause your customers or prospects to accept you quicker. They'll relax and communicate with you in an easier manner. They'll be subconsciously drawn to you.

You'll then develop greater and greater confidence in approaching people. This will, in time, negate a lot of fear of rejection or call-reluctance. The main cause of call-reluctance is our natural fear that we'll go in and look dumb or won't know how to respond in an intelligent way. And since call-reluctance is the main killer of salespeople, and the chief contributor to poverty of salespeople, these ideas will put money in your pockets!

Remember also: don't begin selling, telling, or demonstrating until you successfully develop rapport.

Practicing the ideas in this chapter will help you get people to unlock their mental gates and let you in!

APPROACH Action Guides to Practice This Week

1. Tune the world out and your prospects in.
2. Put them at ease and make them feel important.
3. Get them talking about themselves.
4. Hold eye contact and listen to how they feel.

APPROACH Action Guides to Practice This Week

1. Tune the world out and your prospects in.
2. Put them at ease and make them feel important.
3. Get them talking about themselves.
4. Hold eye contact and listen to how they feel.

Willingham's Wisdom

There was once a hungry salesperson named Barrymore.
Who bored customers by talking until their ears were sore!
    He'd never get to first base,
    Because he didn't have the grace,
To precede his selling by establishing rapport!

(No jealousies, Demosthenes?)

Chapter Three

INTERVIEW—
How to Find Out
Where People Hurt
So You'll Know What
Medicine to Prescribe!

The interview step helps your prospects identify, clarify, and verbalize their wants or needs, thereby revealing to you the conditions upon which they'll buy what you're selling. The interview step is probably the most important of all the six steps of my system of selling. When it's done right, the demonstration, validation, negotiation, and close will all fall into place more easily.

I'll admit that if you'd ask 100 salespeople what they think is the most important part of the sales process, most would say, "The close!"

And, of course, the close is very important—to make something happen is the purpose of the whole process.

But very often when you fail to close, or when you encounter stalls or objections, it's because you didn't successfully carry out the interview step. It's because you never really understood their wants or needs. You never got on their wavelength.

WHEN YOUR INTERVIEW IS EFFECTIVE, YOUR PROSPECTS BEGIN TO SELL THEMSELVES!

One of the exciting features of this system is that when the interview step is successful, your prospects begin to sell themselves.

When they tell you their needs, they're inviting you to show them what you've got that will fill them. They'll often have fewer objections. They'll be more open to closing. Do the interview step right, and your prospects will operate more in the role of selling themselves.

A successful interview accomplishes these three objectives:

1. It gets your prospects talking and you listening—this sets the stage for the most effective persuasion that can take place.

2. The prospects verbalize their needs or wants—this tells you what it'll take to sell them.

3. Your prospects clarify in their own minds what their needs or wants actually are—they commit themselves to you.

Before we get into our action guides, let me tell you a story that illustrates the interview process. I was going over some manuscripts one day when a friend, B. R. Barfield, came into my office.

"What are you working on?" he asked.

"A new sales system."

"New?" he asked curiously. "What is it, and how is it new?"

"It's a simple, systematic approach to selling. It helps make selling more scientific. It's a six-step system that helps people better understand the sales process. The system shows them where they are with a prospect and what to do next. It gives them a track to run on."

"That's interesting. Tell me more."

"Well, I call it need-fulfillment selling. It's a little different philosophy in that it puts the salesperson in an interviewing or consultative role."

"A consultative role?"

"Yes. The steps are, first, to gain rapport with prospects. Then, next, through the use of need-development questions, find out what their needs are.

"What makes this different from conventional sales methods is that the prospect is immediately drawn into an interactive process. The prospect does most of the talking— the salesperson mostly asks questions and listens. But the salesperson remains in control."

"I see," he remarked.

I could see the wheels spinning in his head.

"I've sold that way for years," he said.

"You have?"

"Yes!"

"For instance, remember back when the Strategic Air Command Wing moved into the air base here?"

"Yeah."

"Well, they were going to have to have several-hundred new homes for the Air Force personnel who were moving into town. I was in the homebuilding business then.

"Homebuilders were invited up to Rapid City, South Dakota, to set up shop and sell homes. We all had space in a large hangar there. I sold around fifty homes! Right on the spot! Sight unseen! Want'a know how I did it?"

"Sure."

"Well, I had eight different floor-plans I could build. The usual way to sell would have been to have beautiful pictures and floor-plan layouts blown up and displayed. This way people could walk around and look at them and see what was available. But I didn't do it the usual way."

"You didn't?"

"No. I set up a card table. I sat behind it with two chairs in front of it. Beside me was a sample case filled with pictures and layouts of the different designs I built.

"When people came up, I'd introduce myself and ask them to sit down. I'd spend a few moments getting acquainted.

"I'd ask their names; where they'd lived; how many children they had—questions like that. As they talked, I'd write the information on a pad. I'd make notes of the children's names, ages, and sex.

"I wouldn't ask them what kind of home they wanted— I wouldn't ask them direct questions like that."

"You wouldn't?"

"No, I'd ask them indirect questions such as: 'How often do you entertain?' 'How many people at a time?' 'How many cars do you own?' 'How often do you have overnight guests?' I'd ask them questions such as: 'What do you like most about your present home?' 'What do you like least about it?' 'Do you like a central-entry hall?' 'Do you like a "U"-shaped kitchen?'

"Sometimes I'd ask, 'If you could describe the perfect home for you, what would it be?'

"As they answered these questions," he went on, "I'd make notes. Then when I felt I had enough information about their needs, I'd reach into my briefcase and pull out the one plan that I felt would best suit their needs.

"And you know what?" he asked, looking at me and pausing to make me wait for his point—obviously pleased with the point he was about to make.

"What?" I asked.

He leaned forward, looked into my eyes, tapped my desk, and said, "Everyone except two people bought the plan I showed!"

"Amazing!" I said.

"That's the way I sell," he concluded.

IDENTIFY YOUR PROSPECTS' WANTS OR NEEDS

My friend's example explains the heart of my selling system. The interview step identifies the prospects' wants or needs. It helps you sell without pressure. By using it, you're able to neutralize objections before they come up. It helps deepen your rapport with your prospects. And, as I've said before, it helps put them in the role of selling themselves.

Again, since the emphasis of this book is on doing, here are four action guides for you to practice. Practicing them will help you successfully handle the interview step. The action guides are:

1. Ask open-ended, indirect questions that draw out wants or needs.
2. Listen to and paraphrase all points—write them down.
3. Identify dominant wants or needs—get prospects' agreement.
4. Assure them that you want to help them select the right product or service.

Let's think about these four action guides in detail.

ASK OPEN-ENDED, INDIRECT QUESTIONS THAT DRAW OUT WANTS OR NEEDS

Let me introduce a term that'll play a very prominent role in my sales system. The term is "need-development questions." Need-development questions are open-ended, indirect questions that draw out the wants or needs of your prospects. An open-ended question is one that calls for an explanation. Usually it includes one of these six helpers; "who," "what," "where," "why," "when," or "how." The objective is to get your prospects responding—opening up and talking about their wants or needs

One of the tip-offs of your professionalism is the way you ask these questions. It's important that you ask them so your prospects feel comfortable answering them. You don't want to appear to be prying or squeezing out answers. Nor do you want to threaten another person's comfort zone. If your questions are too direct or abrupt, people will close up instead of opening up. Besides all that, many people feel uncomfortable when you ask them direct, probing questions.

NEED-DEVELOPMENT QUESTIONS

Let me share with you some need-development questions that I've helped some of my clients structure. My objective is for you to understand what need-development questions are, and then for you to structure your own that fit your product or service.

I've trained Army recruiters who're selling career opportunities as well as educational assistance. Since their market is graduating high-school seniors, they talk directly to the students, parents, and school personnel.

NEED-DEVELOPMENT QUESTIONS
ARE OPEN-ENDED AND INDIRECT!

Notice the indirect, open-ended nature of these need-development questions:

"If you had a $5,000 bonus now, what would you do with it?"

"What different jobs or vocations have you thought you'd like the most?"

"If you could travel anywhere in the world and work, where do you think you'd like to go?"

"If you were to decide to go to college, where would the funds come from?"

See how these need-development questions cause a person, in this case a high-school senior, to think, and respond, and begin to verbalize his or her needs?

Notice that the recruiter didn't ask, "Do you want to join the Army?" That would be too direct.

Notice, also, that each question was geared to a benefit—benefits like initial-enlistment bonus, variety of jobs and locations, and college-assistance funds.

By asking these need-development questions and then listening, the recruiters begin to understand what the student really is looking for. And so does the student understand better what he or she is looking for. Then, once the recruiters understand what the students are looking for, they can demonstrate the best plan to help fill the students' wants or needs.

Or, suppose you're selling tires in a retail store. Here are some need-development questions I've trained salespeople to ask:

"What kind of car do you drive?"

"How many miles per year do you drive?"

"How much longer do you plan to keep your car?"

"What kind of driving do you do—in town or on the highway?"

"Are you looking for long wear or low initial cost?"

"What kinds of weather and road conditions do you encounter?"

"Who else rides with you?"

Again, see how these questions are indirect? They're not direct. A direct question would be, "What kind of tires are you looking for?"

STRUCTURE YOUR OWN NEED-DEVELOPMENT QUESTIONS

Now, the trick is to structure your own need-development questions. I suggest that you take the time to polish and refine six most-used questions. Some that you'll use as often as you sell.

I wish you and I had an hour to sit down together and work out your list. In just a moment, I want you to stop your reading, get a pad of paper and a pen, and write out some need-development questions.

ASK "WHO," "WHAT," "WHERE," "WHY," "WHEN," "HOW?"

The secret is to ask "who," "what," "where," "why," "when," or "how" questions that bring you information about your prospects' wants or needs; information such as would be received in reply to the sample questions.

To help you design your own need-development questions, you might first write down what needs your customers have that you can help them fill. Once you've done this, then design specific questions that will draw out the needs you listed.

You might assume the role of a physician. When you go to a doctor, he doesn't ask you, "What's your illness, and what prescription do you need to cure it?"

No, he asks indirect questions about symptoms. Then when he has enough information, he'll make the diagnosis and prescribe a cure. You, too, can operate in the same professional way.

Now, will you please stop and work on some of your own need-development questions? Then come back to this point.

Thank you! If you've followed my suggestion and written out your own need-development questions, you've got something that's worth pure gold! Keep refining them and using them until you have a series of questions that pop into your mind whenever the situation calls for it.

Remember—don't directly ask your prospects what their wants or needs are. Instead, ask them indirect questions that give you information. Then, after you've received the information, you're in a position to professionally determine what their wants and needs are.

Here's a good point to remember: don't ask your customers what they want to buy, but find out their needs, and then recommend what would be their best buy!

Remember too, that you may know, or think you know, what your prospects' wants or needs are. And since you think you know, you're itching to get on with your selling or demonstrating.

But there's more to the interview step than just your learning their wants or needs. The main purpose is for your prospects to *admit* their wants or needs. In doing this, they clarify and define their own problems and build an inner tension for solutions.

Stop a moment, re-read, and think about this statement! It's very important! The more your prospects talk, and you really listen, the more they'll sell themselves. And, the more they'll trust you.

So, let 'em talk!

LISTEN TO AND PARAPHRASE ALL POINTS— WRITE THEM DOWN!

As your prospects talk about their wants or needs, occasionally paraphrase what they say. Paraphrase by summarizing back to them the wants or needs they tell you.

For example, suppose your prospect said, "We have four children so we're looking for a station wagon." Your paraphrase might be something such as, "I understand how a station wagon would give you plenty of room for your four children!"

Paraphrasing also lets you mention a benefit that corresponds to their expressed need. "Plenty of room" is a benefit statement that is a natural one for "four children and a station wagon." When you paraphrase, you let them know that you listened to them, that you understood them, and that what they said was important.

Another professional thing to do is to make notes of what your prospects say. This shows them that you're interested, and that you want to be helpful. Your paraphrasing also helps your prospects further clarify their needs in their own minds. It's a terrific way to deepen rapport and trust with your prospects.

IDENTIFY DOMINANT WANTS OR NEEDS— GET PROSPECTS' AGREEMENT

As you move through the interview step, you'll want to weigh each response and determine which are the dominant wants or needs of your prospects.

To do this, listen carefully to what they say as you ask need-development questions. Then after you feel you've asked enough questions and have enough information to be able to determine their wants or needs, begin to prioritize.

In identifying dominant wants or needs, watch your prospects' body language, eyes, and responses. They'll give you clues as to which of their expressed needs are most valued by them.

Then, to clarify, you can simply ask, "If I understand you correctly, you're saying that your most important needs are to have an automobile large enough for your children as well as to take on camping trips to the mountains?

"Does this sound as if I'm on the right track?" you may ask in order to get feedback.

Asking questions such as these elevates you to the role of a sales counselor rather than a slick, impersonal operator. It sets you apart from salespeople who don't really care what the prospect buys as long as he or she buys something.

In this mode of professionalism, your customers will have more confidence and trust in you. You'll stand out in their minds as someone who's interested in them.

DETERMINE DOMINANT BUYING MOTIVES

The reasons people buy things usually fall into these four categories:

1. Pride
2. Profit
3. Pleasure
4. Peace

These dominant-buying motives are why your prospects will buy from you.

In need-fulfillment selling it helps to understand *why* people buy in order to understand *what* they'll buy.

Pride has to do with how it will make them look to others. How they'll look compared with the "Joneses."

Profit has to do with gain, more dollars in the bank, more financial security, and the promise of profits.

Pleasure has to do with gratifying desires, enjoying a better lifestyle, and having things.

Peace has to do with security and freedom from loss. Peace-of-mind is a strong motivator, as well as relieving tension, removing threats, and insuring the future.

Remember these reasons people buy and try to determine each prospect's dominant buying motive.

EFFECTIVE INTERVIEWING STRENGTHENS TRUST LEVEL!

Your ability to achieve a trust level will be quite a contrast with many of the other salespeople your prospects have dealt with before. Many salespeople try to sell people whatever they appear to like—never really trying to fit their wants and needs with the right product. How often have you gone in to buy clothes—the salesperson asks you what size you wear and then leads you to the rack where your size selection is. Whatever you seem to like, he or she will try to sell it to you.

But, occasionally, you'll find pros who'll first ask you what you're looking for. Then they'll ask for what occasion, where, or when you'll wear it. Maybe they'll ask what image you want to communicate, after which they'll attempt to help you select the appropriate clothes to help you reach your goals

I haven't bumped into too many pros like this. But when I do, I usually find that they're well-rewarded. People trust them, seek them out, and go back again and again.

ASSURE THEM THAT YOU WANT
TO HELP THEM SELECT THE
RIGHT PRODUCT OR SERVICE

Your prospects or customers will usually sense your genuine interest in them. They may even be shocked by it. It's not the most common trait that salespeople demonstrate—unfortunately.

When you *honestly want* to serve your clients in the most meaningful way, you'll naturally assure them both physically and verbally. Your eye contact will be more direct. You'll tune your customers in and other things out. They'll know it! They will, if you're sincere about it.

I've had salespeople tell me that the clothing I was looking at just wasn't right for me, and that another item would serve me much better. I appreciate their time and desire to help me select the right thing. Don't we all?

QUESTIONS, QUESTIONS, QUESTIONS

Questions are the most effective tool a salesperson can use! They can serve you in many ways. With them, you can draw out people, warm them up and break the ice. You can find out what they want and what they're thinking. With questions you can avoid clashes, arguments and head-on collisions.

There are several types of questions. Closed-ended questions ask for a "yes" or a "no" response rather than for an explanation. They usually close up conversation rather than open up conversation. In addition, they usually don't get much information.

Most of the time you'll avoid using closed-ended questions early in your interview, because you don't want to risk getting "no" responses.

Think of some typical exchanges that often take place on a typical sales floor.

"Hello there," Charlie Salesperson says, "may I help you?"

"No, I'm just looking," the prospect says.

"O.K., well, just make yourself at home," the salesperson responds, immediately sensing that this person is a visitor rather than a prospect.

And so both are turned off.

If you think I'm over-simplifying this transaction, you don't have to go into too many retail stores or new-car showrooms to hear this really bright approach. Walk in and open the door on the driver's side and lickety-split, there'll be a voice saying, "Can I fix you up with that little number today?"

Even if you're drooling at the mouth to make a deal, guess what your response will be—99 times out of 100? Right! Your response will be, "Uh, no, I'm just lookin' today."

Then the typical salesperson will tell himself that he spotted you for a flake the moment he saw you, turn around, go back, and shoot the bull with his buddies. Meanwhile, you're standing there wishing he'd taken an interest in you and given you some information in a nonpressured way.

Am I being too hard on "typical" salespeople? Well, maybe. But you'll have to admit there's a lot of truth in what I say. My point, again, is to be careful about how you use questions that call for a "yes" or "no." Don't set yourself up for "no" answers.

REFLECTIVE AND DIRECTIVE QUESTIONS!

Other types of questions we can ask are "reflective" and "directive" ones. A reflective question is designed to cause a person to think, to see more than just one angle.

"After all, your family's safety should come first, shouldn't it?"

"After all, value is measured by more things than just the initial price, wouldn't you agree?"

"I'm sure you'll agree that there's more to consider than merely the price."

"It may be an old cliché, but 'service remains long after the price is forgotten' is still pretty good advice. Wouldn't you say so?"

Questions like these make your prospects think, reflect, and consider more than one line of thought.

A directive question is one that causes prospects to channel their thoughts in a specific direction.

"Don't you agree that with inflation going up and your ability to write off your taxes, a new home is one of the wisest investments you can make, even with high interest rates?"

This is an example of a directive question. It helps move a person's mind in a specific direction.

Another purpose of a directive question would be to help someone sort out and begin making decisions. Such questions as, "What are the most important features that you're looking for in a new car?" or "What color appeals most to you?" are effective.

You can use both reflective and directive questions as "nail-downs" as you're prioritizing prospects' needs or as you're moving toward a close. Usually, you'll want to use them after you've identified their wants and needs with need-development questions. These directive questions are much like trial-close questions in that they bring back opinions and information without asking for a decision. We'll think much more about trial-close questions in later chapters.

So, remember, reflective questions cause a person to think. Directive questions cause people to channel their thoughts in a specific direction—to begin to sort out.

SUMMING UP

I began this chapter by saying that the interview step is probably the most important of all six steps of my system of selling. Let me also say that the interview step is very difficult. It's hard to develop good need-development questions. It's also hard to develop the habit of skillfully using them. I find myself violating my own advice often. I revert to stimulus-response selling too often. I begin selling, telling or demonstrating *before* I identify need; before I allow my prospects or customers to verbalize and talk about their needs. I catch myself thinking, "I already know what their needs are so why waste time?"

But, even when we think we know our customers' needs or wants, it's psychological dynamite to get them talking about them—and us listening!

Remember, a good interview accomplishes these objectives:

1. It gets your prospects talking and you listening—this sets the stage for the most effective persuasion possible.
2. Your prospects verbalize their needs or wants—this tells you what it'll take to sell them.
3. Your prospects clarify in their own minds what their wants or needs actually are—they commit themselves to you.

You can strengthen your interviewing skills by practicing the four action guides that are listed on the next page.

In the interview step, your prospects should spend at least twice as much time talking as you do—you should spend twice as much time listening. But you maintain control because of the questions you ask. Remember—asking questions and listening may work miracles for your sales success!

Remember—before you can prescribe the proper medicine for your prospects, you must first know where they hurt!

INTERVIEW

Action Guides to Practice This Week

1. Ask open-ended, indirect questions that draw out wants or needs.
2. Listen to and paraphrase all points—write them down.
3. Identify dominant wants or needs—get prospects' agreement.
4. Assure them that you want to help them select the right product or service.

Willingham's Wisdom

There was once a starving salesperson named Ralph,
Whose income was somewhat of a drought.
    But his sales began to glisten,
    When he learned to ask questions and listen,
Instead of constantly running off at the mouth!

                  (Wisdom you should know, Plato!)

Chapter Four

DEMONSTRATE—
How to Put More Sell
in Your Show and Tell!

In the early 1960s when I was in the retail-furniture business, my wife and I won trips to the Scandinavian countries. The people, countryside, and cities were scrubbed-up, clean, and beautiful. The beauty of their furniture and household accessory designs excited me. Beautiful flowers bloomed everywhere. The people were friendly and pleasant. The food was inexpensive and delicious.

I'd never ridden in a Mercedes-Benz automobile. Over there they were everywhere. Most of the taxicabs were Mercedes diesels.

I fell in love with them. So as soon as I got back home, I went out to a dealer who had one in stock. Man, I thought it was classy! When I opened and closed a door, it sounded as solid as a bankvault. Everything was quality.

The salesman eyeballed me for several minutes and, I suppose, finally decided that I might be a prospect. So he came over and asked if I'd like to go for a ride in it.

I said I would, and so he motioned for me to get in on the passenger side—which wasn't exactly what I wanted to happen. I got the feeling that he couldn't trust a clod like me with such a fine machine. I wasn't overly impressed with him either!

It didn't take long to see that this guy should've been an engineer instead of a salesman. He was fascinated with all the gadgets and technical data. He got his jollies by demonstrating how you could cram the drive selector into "park" while driving 30 to 40 miles per hour.

While I certainly admired that feature, I couldn't, for the life of me, get all that excited about it.

He demonstrated this to me several times in only a matter of minutes. He explained things like the cubic liters of displacement (whatever that is!). He bored me with the gauge of steel, steering ratio, and other features that didn't exactly send me into ecstasy.

Every time I touched something, he'd almost slap my hand away and do it himself. Not once did he offer to let me drive the car! It burned me up that he had all the fun, and all I got to do was sit there. He never asked my name. Hardly noticed that I was riding with him.

Guess who didn't buy a car from him? You got it!

But guess who found out when that salesman went to lunch, and who went back a couple of days later and bought the car?

I got a different salesman who put me in the driver's seat and let me have all the fun. He made me feel that I was important enough to drive a fine car like that. And I bought!

I've remembered this experience many times during the twenty plus years since it happened. I've learned several lessons from the experience, especially lessons about effective demonstrations.

So this chapter is about demonstrations. How to put more sell in your show and tell!

DON'T BEGIN DEMONSTRATING UNTIL YOU'VE ESTABLISHED NEEDS OR WANTS

The one most-violated principle in selling is that salespeople begin demonstrating before they thoroughly establish what their prospects want or need. I mentioned this fact in the last chapter on interviewing, but it's worth repeating. If you don't believe me, analyze the next ten salespeople who call on you. Walk into a store, shop, or showroom, and most salespeople will tell you about their product's features before they ever ask you need-development questions.

Go into a clothing store. The salesperson will probably show you what's available in your size rather than ask questions to find out what you want, where you're going to wear it, and what kind of *image* you want to project.

Walk into a model home and see how many salespeople properly interview you. Most will begin showing you through the home immediately. So allow me to be negative and say: "Don't begin demonstrating until you've established needs or wants."

PURPOSE OF THE DEMONSTRATION

The purpose of any demonstration is to show how your product or service will answer your prospects' wants or needs.

Remember this simple definition, and you'll make more meaningful demonstrations. An effective demonstration happens when you and your prospects do something together that helps them better understand how your product or service will fill their wants or needs.

A demonstration is most effective when you and your prospects do it *together*. The more personally involved your prospects are, the more effective your demonstration is.

ACTION GUIDES TO HELP YOU DEMONSTRATE MOST EFFECTIVELY

Here are four action guides you can practice to help your demonstrations be most effective. Copy them onto an index card, carry it with you all this week, and let it remind you to practice the four guides at every opportunity.

The action guides are:

1. Repeat prospects' dominant wants or needs.
2. Demonstrate the product or service that will answer them.
3. Avoid talking about price—make it secondary to finding out what best fills their needs.
4. Ask for their reactions, feelings, or opinions.

Now, let's think about each of these action guides in more detail.

REPEAT PROSPECTS' DOMINANT WANTS OR NEEDS

Remember, in the interview step you get your prospects to verbalize their wants or needs. In verbalizing them, they clarify their own thinking and give you a chance to listen and reinforce them. They also give you information about their buying motives... if you'll listen!

You're never ready to go to the demonstration step until you understand their dominant buying motives—the real reason why they'll buy, or the main need they want filled.

Once you feel you understand their dominant buying motives, you're ready to begin the demonstration step.

The first step is to repeat their dominant wants or needs. You can do this with simple statements or questions such as:

"Do I understand you in that what you want most in a new typewriter is durability, and one that will print beautiful, error-free letters at a very high speed?"
or

"Do I understand that what you want most in an automobile is fuel economy as well as safety?"
or

"What's important to you is to be able to wear a suit on an airplane and still arrive looking fresh and crisp for business appointments. Am I correct?"

The secret here is to *summarize* your prospects' dominant want or need and *get agreement* before you move on to the actual demonstration.

This is a very important part in completing the necessary steps that'll lead up to a close.

DEMONSTRATE THE PRODUCT OR SERVICE THAT WILL ANSWER WANTS OR NEEDS

I realize that demonstrations will vary depending upon what you're selling. You may sell products, or services, or ideas, tangibles that people can see, feel, touch, or taste, or intangibles that people have to conceptualize.

But, regardless of what you're selling, here are some basics that'll help you put more sell in your demonstrations:

1. Get your prospects involved.
2. Appeal to both their logic and emotions.
3. Position yourself correctly.
4. Choose the best environment.

Now, let's think briefly about each suggestion.

GET YOUR PROSPECTS INVOLVED

The first Mercedes salesman didn't know how to do this. So he lost a sure sale! If he'd put me in the driver's seat and let me fiddle with the gadgets—he'd have made a sale. I've often wondered how many other sales he lost because he didn't look at selling from the customer's viewpoint.

Speaking of involvement, several years ago my wife and I were invited to a cookware party at some friends' home. Frankly, I was irritated at having to go. But it was a situation we couldn't gracefully get out of. I didn't view going to a cookware party as something that fit my self-image. I agreed to go but didn't promise to either enjoy it or act civilly.

As it turned out, however, it was a most productive evening from several standpoints.

When we arrived, I saw the most stumbling, fumbling person I'd ever seen. This guy had almost no confidence. He dropped lids, misplaced food items, and apologized everytime he turned around. He was one of the most insecure people I'd ever encountered.

At first, I was incensed at having to spend an evening like this. But then a very interesting thing happened. It became so obvious that this salesman was going to have a tough time putting everything together that, without anyone being conscious of it, we all pitched in and helped. He showed his gratitude very openly. Within a few minutes, he was orchestrating the whole show and we were doing all the work.

It was hilarious!

Whether he realized it or not, he had us selling ourselves. He showed us how his stainless-steel pans were so strong that they'd ruin an aluminum pan when banged together. Or course, he didn't do the banging. We were afraid to let him. So one of us did.

He also got one of the wives scrubbing an aluminum pan with steel wool—to show the grey, yukky color that resulted. All of us gagged at having something like that going into our stomachs. We all praised the meal "he'd fixed" for us—afraid that if we didn't his self-esteem would suffer more damage.

When he got to the end of the meeting, his close was pathetic. He could hardly explain how to fill out the order torm. Finally we had to look at it, decide what went where, and "help" him figure it out.

Of course we all bought! We couldn't have lived with ourselves if we'd rejected such a weak person! It would've been like stomping baby chickens, or running down decrepit grandmother pedestrians!

A few days later when he delivered our set, I asked him how many of the people there bought.

"Oh, everyone," he responded. "All five couples."

"Well, how many of these meetings do you hold each week?" I asked him.

He appeared to be reluctant to have to admit how few he held, explaining that he wasn't doing as well as he should, had some past-due bills to pay off, and needed a better car.

"Only about two a week," he said, fumbling with the delivery receipt, trying to figure out which one he left with me. Like a mother hen, I helped him out when he asked if I could figure out which one he should leave me. Thanking me, he left.

After he left, I got to figuring out how much he made. "On a $450 sale, he's bound to make $300 commission. He sold five sets the other night. That's...$1500. He does this twice a week. That's...$3,000 per week times four. Great Day! That's $12,000 per month. That's several times more than I make in my furniture store! And I've got a big investment!"

Well, my point is to get your prospects involved! Get them selling themselves. It'll pay off big for you!

APPEAL TO BOTH THEIR LOGIC AND EMOTIONS

My experience is that people have two agendas when buying:

1. The reasons they give you for buying

2. The hidden, real reasons

Most people will pretend they're buying out of a logic base—for good, sound, logical reasons. But the more I sell, the more I'm convinced that emotional reasons influence buyer decisions much more than logic.

Not to stomp our poor Mercedes salesman to death, but he tried to sell me with logic—talking about technical, engineering data. And I couldn't have cared less at what tolerance the engine parts were milled.

I wanted the car because I thought it was classy and different. None of my friends had one. It'd take curves and corners fast and float over dips and bumps. I liked the feel of its steering wheel. I felt safer in it. It was comfortable. The radio was neat! The dash was real wood!

If he'd been observant or taken the time to ask, he could've easily determined my buying motives.

Whatever you're selling, there are logical reasons why people buy and there are emotional reasons. Let's say that you're selling insurance. The logical reason a person would buy might be to save money; the emotional reason might be protection from loss or to appear more responsible.

I've helped train security-alarm salespeople. The logical appeal to homeowners is that it makes good sense to protect their valuables.

A more emotional appeal would be to get them visualizing their important, irreplaceable valuables stolen; or thinking about what they'd do if they walked into their home and interrupted a robbery; or visualizing the possibility of attackers or burglars breaking in while they're home.

In selling automobile tires, the logical appeal would be longwear and miles-per-dollar invested. The emotional appeal would be the steelbelted construction and tread design that would help protect your wife or loved ones from bad weather or from having a flat out on a dark, lonely road.

In using logic, you show the good sense of investing in your product or service.

In using emotion, you get the prospects visualizing themselves enjoying having it or enjoying how it will make them look to others; or you help create mental pictures in their minds of suffering from suddenly needing it and not having it.

Here are some suggestions for appealing to people's emotions as you demonstrate: get them feeling; get them tasting; get them looking; get them doing; and get them experiencing.

Get them emotionally experiencing the rewards of having your product or service. Get them experiencing the shock or loss of not having it.

Ask for feedback as you demonstrate. Ask them how they feel about it, how they like it, and how it looks to them.

Use vivid word pictures that help them visualize themselves enjoying the benefits of your product or service.

The more you adapt these ideas to what you're selling, the more successful you'll become in influencing buyer behavior in your demonstrations.

POSITION YOURSELF CORRECTLY

Another important technique of demonstrating is to learn to use dominant and subordinate positions. Let's think about where you position yourself as you're demonstrating. The reason I bring this up is that it's very important to respect your prospects' space. In demonstrating, you want them to feel comfortable with you. You don't want them to feel threatened.

People may not want you to get too close or become too familiar with them. So be careful.

Studies have shown that men usually want to keep salesmen just over an arm's length away. A saleswoman can get closer if she's selling to another woman. A man can move in slightly, often, when selling to a woman.

Also, studies show that right-hand buyers want salespeople standing just to their left-of-center.

When the demonstration involves something both of you can hold, look at, or do together, you can get closer to your prospects than you might otherwise be able to do.

When they concentrate on what you're demonstrating, they'll not be so concerned or aware of your position. Their fear of you or fear of what you're going to do to them also lessens.

As you're demonstrating, put your eyes and point where you want them to put their eyes. Consciously move at their speed. March to their cadence! Then gradually pick up your tempo. See if they don't, then, begin to march to your cadence.

These actions help develop stronger bonding and rapport. You'll cement trust relationships quicker.

If you're selling a committee, board, or group, get the boss or strongest decision-maker helping you. Have her or him hold charts, flip slides, write on a chalkboard, or do other active things. Position yourself so the decision-maker's sitting with you as you demonstrate to the "others." Ask the decision-maker to help you field some of the questions that come up. Get her or him on your side, helping you to "sell the others."

CHOOSE THE BEST ENVIRONMENT

Often customers or prospects build power structures or protective devices into their environments. They structure dominant positions and put you in subordinate positions.

I've seen buyers' offices in which the guests' seating was far enough from the desk so that it protected the buyer. I've seen them have sofas or lower chairs for guests. This causes the salesperson to sit lower; thus creating a power position for the buyer.

Distractions, in homes or offices, can put you in a weaker position. Television sets turned on in homes can create a poor-selling environment. Other people jammed around a buyer, in a business setting, can create problems during your demonstration.

I called on a man in the Department of Labor once to sell some job-training seminars. He was a typical social type—jolly, friendly, and easy to get to know. Two minutes after I met him, we were big buddies. I thought I had a big sale wrapped up. I noticed that he started fidgeting and glancing at his watch.

Then in a few minutes, in the middle of my sentence, he bolted from his chair, ran over to the window, picked up a long telescope, and peered through it at the street where a covey of secretaries was walking to lunch.

When I heard the sound effects and saw the silly grin on his face, I knew two things: one, that my interview had crashed; and, two, how my tax dollars were being spent!

Well, if you sell in people's natural environment—home or office—get them into the friendliest and least-distracting part. More sales are made around the kitchen table than anywhere else in homes. It's an excellent demonstrating place. Lots of products are sold to purchasing agents in the coffee shop, during lunch, or on the golf course. So, always try to choose carefully the best selling environment.

AVOID TALKING ABOUT PRICE

Price is not important until you find out what your prospects want or need. One of the most common traps that salespeople fall into is giving price information *before* they get the prospects' agreement that they want what's being demonstrated. It's very common to get price questions early in a sales interview. It's here that many salespeople get killed. They get killed if they fall into the trap of answering.

A good way to handle premature price questions is to say, "I understand how you're interested in the price, but before we even think about the price, let's make sure that we find what best fills your needs!"

Then, if you think it's worthwhile, springboard to an information-getting question such as, "But, while we're thinking about price, what general price range do we need to stay in?"

Listen carefully to them. Let them know that you want to help them select the best *value*. Let them know that value is determined by comparing price with satisfaction and service.

Now, I realize that you can't always skirt price questions at this point. But try the above two strategies. See how they work for you. They can become very handy tools to help you at this rough and sticky spot.

ASK FOR THEIR REACTIONS, FEELINGS, OPINIONS

Big-league, customer-centered salespeople constantly draw out their prospects. Not only does feedback allow you to know where you are with your prospects, but it's a powerfully persuasive activity.

Learn to solicit opinions. "What do you think?" "How do you feel about this feature?" "How important is this feature to you?" "Which features appeal most to you?" "What other features do we still need to consider?"

As you ask these questions, listen to what your prospects' words say. Listen to what their expressions say. Listen to what their body language says. Listen to what their emotions say.

Asking these kinds of questions during your entire demonstration causes your prospects to lower their resistances; to give you valuable information, to sell themselves, and to clarify in their own minds what they want.

It also gives you a chance to listen and give them all kinds of positive feedback. Your feedback shows that you're concerned and interested. This is a powerful principle of persuasion.

Remember...you don't *talk* people into buying; you *listen* them into buying!

WHY PEOPLE WILL BUY YOUR PRODUCT
OR SERVICE

Here are two simple facts that have helped me better understand buyer motivation. People will buy your product or service for two reasons:

1. What it will *do* for them

2. How it will make them *look* to others

It's important to understand buyer motivation. People buy to fill wants or needs; to enjoy satisfaction or to protect from loss. Obviously, there's a difference between wants and needs. Probably more people buy because of wants rather than needs.

We need food, water, and air for survival. But, after we pass the survival stage, our wants are usually stronger than our needs.

We *need* transportation; we may *want* a flashy sportscar or a high-mileage car. We *need* friends; we *want* to be esteemed by others. We *need* food, clothing, and shelter; we *want* to dine out in nice restaurants, have stylish clothes, and live in nice homes in prestigious neighborhoods.

We want enjoyment, satisfaction, and pleasure, as well as security, recognition, and money. We also want to feel good, be healthy, and look good.

SUMMING UP

Now, let's stop a moment and recap what you've read in this chapter.

I gave you several suggestions for putting more sell in your demonstrations. One was: don't begin demonstrating until you've established your prospects' wants or needs. This may be the most-violated rule of selling.

I wrote that the purpose of your demonstration is to show how your product or service will answer your prospects' wants or needs.

You may be able to demonstrate your actual product—such as an automobile, home, clothing, appliances, or other items. Or you may be selling ideas or services; so, you may demonstrate with pictures, charts, graphs, or printed pieces, or in other ways that help your prospects visualize the benefit to them.

Then I gave you four action guides to practice that'll vitalize your demonstrations. You'll see these four guides listed at the end of this chapter.

You'll want to write them on a card and practice them over and over until you do them unconsciously.

I mentioned some tips to remember when demonstrating. They are:

1. Get your prospects involved.
2. Appeal to both their logic and emotions.
3. Position yourself so you don't threaten your buyer.
4. Choose the best environment in which to demonstrate.

Doing these suggestions will help you put more sell in your show and tell!

DEMONSTRATION

Action Guides to Practice This Week

1. Repeat prospects' dominant wants or needs.
2. Demonstrate the product or service that will answer them.
3. Avoid talking about price—make it secondary to finding out what best fills their needs.
4. Ask for their reactions, feelings, or opinions.

Willingham's Wisdom

There was once a struggling salesperson named Snelling,
Who had no emotional appeal in his selling!
    But when he learned in his demonstration
    To appeal to his prospects' imagination,
He now gets them involved tasting, touching, and
smelling!

(Engage your envy, Emerson?)

Chapter Five

VALIDATE—
How to Get People
Nodding Their Heads and Saying,
"By Golly, I Believe This'll
Do What You Say!"

When I was in the retail-furniture business, a big part of our sales volume was upholstered sofas and chairs. Our major line was very well-made and more expensive than most other brands.

Every time we sold an upholstered piece, we not only had to demonstrate it, but we had to *prove* that it would give more value for the dollars invested, that it had superior construction and would wear longer than less-expensive ones. In other words, we had to *validate* our claims! We had to *prove* what we said was true!

One way we did this was to show customers a sample of the framing wood in our sofas and chairs. We'd point out the extra thickness of it, and then, to prove how hard the wood was, we'd use it to drive a nail into another piece of wood. This was a great tension-breaker and attention-getter.

People were always concerned about the wearability of the fabrics. Since most of our fabrics were Scotchgarded, here's how we turned that feature into a customer benefit.

First we'd explain the soil-resistant qualities. Then we'd say, "What this means to you is that when your guests or children soil the fabric, whatever they spill will come right off without penetrating the fibers!"

As we explained how the feature of Scotchgarding helped the piece look better and last longer, we'd demonstrate. We'd ask the customer to pour hot coffee or black ink on a fabric sample. The coffee or ink would bead up and roll around. Then we'd give them some tissues and ask them to blot up the coffee or ink.

This demonstration was always a shocker to people. But it was convincing proof that what we said was true. It proved that our fabrics would resist soiling.

It validated our claims!

EVERYTHING YOU SELL MUST BE VALIDATED!

Everything you sell must be *validated!* You must validate yourself! You must validate your product or service! You must validate your company! Validation isn't so much a separate step that comes after the demonstration, it's really a process that takes place throughout your entire presentation. It does if a sale is going to be made!

While validation is an ongoing process, it's still a step that has to be accomplished before you can successfully negotiate and close.

If your prospects still don't really believe you, or are still resisting you, it's pointless to try for a close. You're going nowhere until you validate your claims—until you get them believing that what you're saying is the truth.

You must get them saying, "By golly, I believe this'll do what you say!"

As I look back at many sales I've missed, I can clearly see this fact: the prospects never really believed my claims.

I remember calling on a school administrator to sell him some self-concept development programs that I'd written. I blew the sale by going from the approach directly to demonstrating. I didn't get him talking about his needs. In the middle of my demonstration, he interrupted, "Do you realize how many people come in here and try to sell me stuff like this?"

When he said, "stuff like this," my ego bristled because I'd written it. Besides all that, it wasn't "stuff." It was new, creative, and very good. In fact, it was great! It would help his teachers build self-esteem in their students, instead of tearing it down—which many do. Well, he wasn't too friendly after I told him the foregoing facts. And I didn't leave any richer.

The truth was that he had nothing in his system that would do what my program would do. The truth was also that he had a strong need for developing stronger self-esteem in children. But, while these things were the truth, I might as well have been selling the Brooklyn Bridge.

I didn't validate it! I didn't cause him to believe that my programs would work for him. And it was my fault, not his!

Stop and think about the importance of validation for a few moments. Analyze your own selling. See if you've missed sales because your prospect never really believed what you claimed.

Here are four action guides that'll help you validate your claims more effectively. Read them carefully, and then we'll spend some time thinking about each one.

1. Translate product features into customer benefits.

2. Justify price and emphasize value.

3. Offer proof-of-benefit claims and satisfied users.

4. Reassure and reinforce prospects to neutralize fear of buying.

TRANSLATE PRODUCT FEATURES INTO CUSTOMER BENEFITS

People don't buy features; they buy benefits. They don't buy what the product or service is. They buy for what it'll *do for* them or for how it'll *make them look* to others. Sure, features are important, but only as they'll benefit your prospects. "What's this going to do for me?" They want to know.

When you buy new clothes, you don't select something because of its thread count per inch, or other technical specifications.

Probably, you buy clothes because they'll wear well, because you'll look good in them, or because of comfort or style.

You don't buy a vacuum cleaner because of the size of the motor or because of the length of the cord. You buy it because it's strong enough to pick up dust and dirt from your floor.

You don't buy a car because of the number of horsepower in the engine or the gauge of steel in the door panel. No, you buy because you want economy or power; or because you love the color or styling; or because you like the feel of the upholstery or the sound of the stereo.

In everything you sell, there are features, and there are benefits. Features are what make up the product or service. Benefits are what it'll do for your prospects—advantages it'll offer them.

It's very common for salespeople to try to sell features rather than benefits because the product features are benefits to them as salespeople.

For example, if you're a life-insurance agent, it's to your benefit to have features in your policies that your competitors don't have. You're excited about having these features because having them benefits you. But these features aren't benefits to your customer until you translate them.

Here's a way to translate your product's features into benefits for your prospects. Learn these six magic words, and you'll eat better.

SIX MAGIC WORDS

The six magic words that'll help you eat better and make more trips to the bank are:

"What this means to you is... "

Whenever you mention a feature, say to your prospects, "What this means to you is...," and then mention how they'll benefit from the feature.

Let me give you a couple of for instances:

"This tire is a steel-belted radial. What this means to you is that it'll wear longer, help save on your gas mileage, and give you the peace-of-mind that you're not as apt to have a flat or blowout while driving."

"After I conduct this sales-training seminar for you, I'll provide you with a six-week follow up. What this means to you is that your salespeople will retain more of what I present them, develop stronger selling habits, and you'll get much more for your training dollar!"

"Mrs. Jones, this home is located in a very desirable neighborhood. What this means to you is that should your husband be transferred, or if you should choose to sell it for other reasons, the chances are that it'll sell faster and bring you top dollar!"

Well, you get the idea. Translate features into benefits. Tell your prospects what your features mean to them. Then add an extra benefit as a clincher.

JUSTIFY PRICE AND EMPHASIZE VALUE

First, let me say that you must *really believe* that the price you're asking is much less than the value your product or service will give your prospects.

Do you believe that the value of what you're selling far exceeds the price you're asking for it? Do you?

The first person you must convince is yourself! And when you believe it—really believe—you'll be able to convince others. You'll have no hesitancy or reluctance to ask for the price. You'll have less fear of price resistance.

But if you don't believe it, your doubts will come through in dozens of ways.

Also, let me play Socrates for a moment and say that if you're just trying to sell something to make a buck, you've got a tough job. It's going to be very tough to validate something you yourself aren't emotionally wrapped-up in.

Well, back to the subject.

Value results when we think of the service, enjoyment, and benefits divided by the price.

Some of the most expensive suits I've bought have been ones that I found on sale. The initial price was cheap, but they didn't fit, look good, or wear well.

They did not represent value!

On the other hand, I've bought expensive suits that looked good, felt good, and wore several times longer than others.

They cost more, sure, but they represented value!

Most buyers are looking for value!

Are they interested in price? Of course, but as it relates to value.

Another way to emphasize value is to break the usage into several minor expenditures: "It's only 30 cents a day for this new calculator." or, "For only the price of a pack of cigarettes and a cup of coffee each day, you can have a savings plan that will be worth $10,000 in fifteen years!"

PRE-ANSWER PRICE OBJECTIONS BEFORE THEY COME UP

Throughout your demonstration and validation steps, you'll want to stack value after value on the scales. You do this so that when you get to the price, the value and benefits will outweigh it in your prospect's mind.

Let me give you an example. I once consulted with a firm that sold security alarms. When they sold and installed an alarm system in a home or office, it was always custom-designed to fit the customer's needs. Since there was an initial installation charge, as well as a monthly fee, their salespeople often encountered price objections.

One way they pre-answered the price objections was in the initial interview. They'd say, "The price that you'll pay for this system will depend on the separate items that go into it."

They'd then go on, "You'll decide the ultimate price by the features you select. If, when we finish designing the system, it's too much, we can take out things until the price is where you want it to be." This usually relaxed their prospects and temporarily stalled the price question.

Then as they designed the system, they'd ask their prospects if they wanted panic buttons at certain doors, motion detectors in certain locations, and other things.

As the prospects agreed on each separate equipment need, the salesperson would write down the price for that item.

When they got through, the salesperson added up the amount—which was what the people had said they wanted. This procedure reduced the impact of the final price. The prospects felt involved in the process. It reduced their price objections.

Well, there are many ways to pre-answer price objections before they come up. Mainly, you do it by stacking up units of value as you go along.

OFFER PROOF-OF-BENEFIT CLAIMS
AND SATISFIED USERS

The third action guide for the validation step is to offer proof-of-benefit claims and satisfied users. Proof letters, testimonials, and third-party letters can be very powerful in validating your claims. Their power, however, hinges on your prospects' identifying with the endorser. Prospects must either know the endorsers or be in a similar business in order for the testimonials to be effective.

I'm not motivated by a newspaper ad that quotes a "Mr. B.," who lives a thousand miles away, as having lost thirty pounds on a diet plan. But I am impressed by someone I've known who lives down the street. I'm also impressed by someone in my same line of work.

So, carefully tailor your proof letters and statements so they'll be most powerful to your prospects. Remember, they must be believable, desirable, and in similar circumstances for your prospects to be influenced by them.

REASSURE AND REINFORCE PROSPECTS TO NEUTRALIZE FEAR OF BUYING

There's an interesting psychological phenomenon that often takes place while people are deciding whether or not to buy. It's called fear! Fear that they'll do the wrong thing—make the wrong decision. Another fear that people have is their natural resistance to change. This fear keeps people from buying, often, when they know they should.

So when you pair these two fears—fear of making a wrong decision and resistance to change—you've got a formidable enemy to deal with. Professional salespeople recognize these two realities. They realize that they're normal. They're equipped to deal with them.

When I sold office and home furnishings, we had to deal with these fears all the time. Since we designed complete interiors—carpets, wall coverings, drapery, and furniture—most clients couldn't visualize how the finished rooms would look. Frequently, items would have to be special-ordered for the client. There were always doubts in people's minds whether their home or office would look good when finished. To deal with this fear, we often did color renderings to show them exactly what it would look like. Or we'd show them other homes or offices that we'd done.

Often people selecting single pieces of furniture would be afraid to make decisions—fearing that they wouldn't be happy once they got the piece home.

To help offset this fear, we'd offer to take the piece to the home or office to let them see how it would look. This took the pressure off them and often removed the fear of making a decision.

Also, since one of their fears was how their friends or neighbors would react to their purchase, we'd often ask them to bring their friend in to see what was being considered. Occasionally this backfired, but it worked more times than not. It was a way of dealing with their fear.

SHARE WHAT IT'S DONE FOR YOU

I've held seminars for people who market Shaklee products. I'd never taken food supplements, but at one seminar, Jim Calvert, who has a doctorate in physiology and has taught in a major university, told me what the supplements had done for him personally.

Upon hearing of his improved health, recognizing his credentials, and having his wife and brother validate his claims, I *believed* and was motivated to begin using them. I did, and feel much better as a result! More stamina! More energy!

A friend of mine, Bernard Petty, has been in the wholesale-gasoline business for several years. A person of outstanding character, he's been very successful. His weight increased little by little over several years until he needed to lose several pounds. He couldn't run because of bad knees, so he discovered a unique exercise unit.

Within a month he began to lose inches and pounds. After three months of exercising and also watching what he ate, he'd lost almost thirty-five pounds and 4½ inches in his waist. Suddenly, his friends began asking him how he did it. When he told them, they wanted to purchase a unit for themselves.

So he began selling the units—at first just to help his friends. But then their friends wanted to buy units. In about four months Bernard sold over 1,000 of these exercise units. It retailed for about $200, so you see the dollars were significant.

His success seemed to spring from the ability of his friends and himself to personally validate the product. And yes, he sold me one, too! In fact, I'm going to stop and get on it now and work out the writer's cramp that's in my brain. . . .

OK, I'm back!

THE NEED FOR SELF-VALIDATION

Some important points are obvious in the examples I've just given, but permit me to emphasize them.

First, you must believe in what you're selling as a value generator. You must be convinced of its integrity. Ford salespeople shouldn't drive Chevrolets. Neither can Ford salespeople honestly validate their product if they change jobs each month—drifting around from dealer to dealer.

Second, you must validate *yourself* to your prospects. They must see you as a person of integrity, honesty, and sincere commitment to giving them value.

Finally, of course, you must validate your product or service—as we've discussed in this chapter.

SHOW THAT YOUR PRODUCT OR SERVICE IS CONSISTENT WITH YOUR PROSPECTS' VALUES OR BELIEFS

The psychology of this is dynamite! You won't hear this taught in many sales meetings or courses. But knowing it and being sensitive to it will put you into a deeper level of sales success.

Here's the point: people subconsciously resist ideas or offerings that aren't consistent with their values or beliefs. To say it another way: people only accept ideas or offerings that they feel are consistent with their values and beliefs.

Let me give you an example. Gene Klein, Jr., called on a family to sell them an alarm system for their home. The initial installation charge was going to be about three thousand dollars.

When it came time to talk about price, the husband balked. He balked because he didn't want to spend that kind of money. What he was unconsciously saying was, "It's not in my value system to spend that much money on an alarm. My money is worth more to me than your alarm system." The man told Gene, "It's not worth that kind of money."

Rather than being stopped, Gene looked at the man's wife and asked, "Is it worth that kind of money to you to know that when your husband is at work or out of town that you're going to be safe from burglars, and that your irreplaceable valuables are going to be protected?"

After saying that, Gene shut his mouth and looked at her.

In a moment she replied, "Yes, it would certainly be worth that much money for my peace-of-mind!" Whereupon Gene silently looked at the husband. After a few painful seconds, the husband took a deep breath and asked, "Where do I sign?"

As you see, whereas before it wasn't consistent with his values to spend three thousand dollars, an overriding value caused him to go ahead; and he acted consistently with the overriding value.

SUMMING UP

To summarize, let me say that validation is *proving* that your product or service will answer your prospects' wants or needs.

Rather than being a step that you do between the demonstration and negotiating steps, it's really an ongoing process—from the beginning of your sale to the close.

You must validate your product or service. You must validate yourself. You must validate your company.

Remember the six magic words that help you translate features into benefits. They are, "What this means to you is. . . ." Memorize these six words and constantly use them in your demonstration and validation.

Constantly be stacking up value on the scales, so that when you get to the price, it'll be totally outweighed. This way you'll pre-answer price objections before they come up.

Recognize that most people have a fear of buying. Always be prepared to reassure them and reinforce them. If you can, share what your product or service has done for you. This is powerful validation.

Remember that your own integrity will be a strong, silent validator.

And finally, recognize the need to show that having your product or service is consistent with your prospects' values or beliefs.

Patiently practice these things and, in time, you'll be more skilled in how to get people to nod their heads and say, "By golly, I believe this'll do what you say!"

VALIDATION

Action Guides to Practice This Week

1. Translate product features into customer benefits.
2. Justify price and emphasize value.
3. Offer proof-of-benefit claims and satisfied users.
4. Reassure and reinforce prospects to neutralize fear of buying.

Willingham's Wisdom

There was once a poor salesperson named Grable,
Who could hardly put beans on the table.
    But steak and lobster she soon ate,
    When her claims she learned to validate,
And now it's all ermine and sable!

(Like these lines, Longfellow?)

Chapter Six

NEGOTIATE—
How to Let Your Customers
Have the Last Word
So They'll Let You Have
Their Last Dollar!

Several years ago, I sold the copyrights and inventory of a program I'd written to another training firm for $250,000. The terms were $25,000 down and $25,000 each six months until paid.

Since the firm had a fairly low net worth, and the president had a very high net worth, we agreed that he'd sign the contract both as president of the firm and as an individual.

When I got the contract back, along with the down payment, it wasn't signed on the line marked, "Individually." When I called the man, he explained that, after thinking it over, he didn't want to be personally liable.

Those weren't the terms of the sale as I'd understood them so I immediately went to see him. He met me at the airport and again explained that should he be personally liable and something happened to him, it would throw a burden on his wife that he didn't want.

I replied that I could appreciate how he felt, and then asked if the possibility of an untimely death was his only reason for not signing it personally. He said that it was the only reason.

I then explained that without his personal guarantee my bank wouldn't accept the contract as collateral should I need to borrow against it—which I probably would do in designing new courses. Then I asked him that if I could guarantee that his wife wouldn't be stuck with the liability should he die an untimely death, would he sign.

"Yes," he said, "if I could guarantee that."

Anticipating this, I had with me an application for a term-insurance policy for $250,000. I gave this to him and told him that I'd pay the premiums for the term of his note. This negotiation solved his problem and solved my problem. We were both happy. It made a win-win situation.

In almost every sales transaction, there is a certain amount of negotiation that has to take place. The negotiation may involve price, terms, or delivery.

Good closers are ultimately good negotiators. Poor closers are usually poor negotiators.

NEGOTIATION CAN BECOME A BATTLE OF EGOS!

Very often when salespeople get to the negotiation step, they allow it to develop into a battle of egos. Their egos clash with their prospects' egos.

Too often, salespeople look at selling as an "I win-you lose" situation. This almost always forces their prospects into viewing it the same way. So they butt heads.

Nowhere else does the ego show itself as much as in the negotiating step. The more I'm in selling, the more I see people's egos influencing the outcomes. Whether a person buys or fails to buy often has more to do with ego than logic.

It took me a long time to learn this fact. I lost a lot of sales before I began to learn it. And, to be honest, I still have to re-learn it from time to time.

Not too long ago, I personally called on the executive officer at an Army District Recruiting Command. I explained to him the sales seminars that I'd done for other recruiting commands around the country. He admitted and talked about his need.

I gave him references to call as well as testimonial letters from other offices. I even suggested that he call the colonel who was his boss at the regional level.

We talked about the price. He had no problem with that. We discussed times, dates, and locations. He was very positive and excited.

He explained that he'd have to clear it with his boss at the district level. I was to call him back in a few days.

When I called him back, I could tell his enthusiasm was still high. He was very friendly and chatty. Almost immediately, I could sense that the sale was approved.

Then he said, "The boss said I'd have to beat you down on your prices before we can go ahead!"

The moment he said, "Beat you down," my ego flared up. I instantly resented what he'd said. Of course, I should've known better. After all, I'm an expert(?)!

Without thinking, I shot back, "I do good work! I don't cut my fees!"

The way I said it put a chill in the air. Then I rushed in where angels fear to tread. I told him that he could get cheaper people, but he couldn't get better ones. That I delivered the goods! That I got results!

Well, even over the telephone I could almost see him tense, grit his teeth, and get ready to come back at me. His voice turned to icicles. He stalled me by saying that he'd have to get back with his boss and ended the conversation very quickly.

After I hung up, I wanted to kick myself for doing what I knew better than to do. I realize that I'd put him in a position of not only having to defend his ego with me, but also with his colonel.

I realized that when he said he'd have to beat me down, I should have countered with a mildly phrased statement. One such as, "I understand how both you and your boss *feel!* Everyone wants to be as thrifty as possible."

Then I should have said, "Most of my other clients *felt* the same way before I worked with them. But most *found* that my seminars get results for them, and that value isn't measured in dollars but in results!"

Well, this is what I should have said! But I didn't! I blew it!

THE FEEL, FELT, FOUND FORMULA

If you'll stop for a moment, you'll see that I should've used these three key words when talking to the major. I should've used the words: "feel," "felt," and "found."

The Feel, Felt, Found Formula can become one of the most valuable tools in your sales-skills kit. Thoroughly learn it and you can use it many, many times. It'll get you out of many jams. It'll help you skirt ego clashes. It'll get prospects on your side.

Use the Feel, Felt, Found Formula each time you get an objection, stall, or put-off. Use it when you meet resistance. Use it when you meet hostility or have to deal with an unhappy customer.

Whenever you get a negative response from people, take a deep breath, look at them in their right eyeballs, and calmly say, "I understand how you *feel*...." Then let them know that others *felt* the same way until they *found* out...(and here inject what they found out that changed their minds). This is one of the most disarming strategies that a salesperson can use.

I've read of Abraham Lincoln's persuasive skills in the courtroom; of how he almost never lost a case, and how he'd never argue or attack an opponent. In fact, the biographer Herndon tells how Lincoln, at first, would argue his opponent's case—telling all the reasons why his opponent was right. He'd appear to agree to all the things his opponent said. He'd tell what a fine person his opponent was.

Then he'd begin bending the minds of the jurors by saying, "While all these things are true, and my opponent has skillfully presented them, there are a few other things that influence this case."

Then he'd begin slowly with his own arguments. He was a master at diplomacy—at getting people to change their minds and feel good doing it.

WIN AN ARGUMENT AND LOSE A SALE!

It's an old cliché, but true nonetheless—win an argument and lose a sale! But it's sales we're after! Right? Who gets a commission check for winning arguments?

One of the best salespeople I know is a man who's softspoken and quiet. When sales get to the negotiation stage, he speaks so softly that his customers almost have to strain to hear him.

For many years I thought that this was the secret of his high closing ratio. But the more I studied him, the more I saw that his secret is in the way he fields objections.

After watching him, I discovered that he carefully listens to the objection, and then nods his head up and down and says, "I can sure understand how you feel!" Then he'll spend several minutes stating their case for them. He'll explain why they're justified in feeling the way they do.

He'll explain that others have felt the same way, that it's even normal to feel that way. That they have a right to feel that way. After all, it's their money, and they should be concerned about getting the most value for it.

After he completely neutralizes their objections, he'll begin telling them that he's giving them value, and it's a wise decision for them to go ahead and buy. Then assuming that they're going to buy, he'll come right out and ask them to do so.

I've watched him deal with some very sticky human relations problems: times when tempers were ready to flare. He'd calmly put his hand on the people's shoulders, look into their eyes, and go through the same neutralizing negotiation. He's probably never heard of the Feel, Felt, Found Formula, but he uses it to perfection.

ONE OF OUR STRONGEST NEEDS IS TO FEEL UNDERSTOOD AND VALUED

Understanding this practical psychology can lead almost anyone to higher sales and earnings. Showing value and understanding to customers is powerfully reinforcing. When we give value and understanding to our prospects, they're instinctively impelled to give value and understanding back to us, to "see things our way." This is the law of psychological reciprocity.

Most people are willing to exchange their objections for our understanding and value. By this, I mean that they'll often "give in" when they feel we really understand, care for, and value them.

They'll almost never "give in" if we put our foot on their throats and try to beat them into submission.

Showing value and understanding usually means we have to subordinate our own egos and look out for our customers' rights as much as for our own.

These may sound like Sunday School ideas; but, in reality, they're deep psychological concepts. They also require a degree of maturity in the salesperson in order to carry them out.

It's worth repeating—people are often willing to change their opinions and positions when they know that we value them, understand how they feel, and grant them the right to feel that way.

ACTION GUIDES TO HELP YOU NEGOTIATE WELL

Here are four action guides to practice and develop into your habit patterns:

1. Ask, "Is there anything that's keeping you from buying now?"
2. Welcome objections—let prospects know that you understand how they feel.
3. Identify specific objections—get agreement that these are the only ones.
4. Discuss possible solutions—ask prospects' opinions for the best solution.

ASK, "IS THERE ANYTHING THAT'S KEEPING YOU FROM BUYING NOW?"

You'd probably never be this direct or blunt and ask the question like I've stated it. You'd want to be much more diplomatic. You'd want to rephrase it to be more subtle and fit the occasion and personality of your prospect. The purpose of the question is to flush out the prospects' objections, and to find out why they are objecting.

We'll talk more about trial-close questions in the next chapter, but this is an excellent place to ask them. A trial-close question is one that asks for an *opinion*! What kind of trial-close questions can you ask to flush out objections?

Well, maybe ones like these:

"At this point, Mr. or Mrs. Prospect, how do you feel about this?

"What are some of your concerns about this filling your needs?

"What reservations do you have that need to be straightened out before going ahead and purchasing this...?

"What are some of the things you like most, and things you like least about this?"

These and similar trial-close questions get needed information for you. They help you flush out real objections.

WELCOME OBJECTIONS—LET PROSPECTS KNOW THAT YOU UNDERSTAND HOW THEY FEEL

Very often objections are buying signals. When people give them, they're often saying, "Here's my condition for buying from you!", or, "I want to buy, but I don't want to give in too easily!" Or they may be saying, "Sell me—give me more information, reinforcement, or reassurance."

Weak salespeople are afraid of objections. They melt when they encounter them. Pros have learned not to overreact to them but treat them in a calm manner. Treating objections in a calm manner often takes the sting out of them. By welcoming objections and asking your prospects to rephrase them, two positive things happen:

1. Objections often diminish when prospects talk them out.
2. You have another chance to listen, show concern, and reinforce your prospects.

Paraphrasing their objections as you use the Feel, Felt, Found Formula has terrific power to neutralize them. For instance, you might ask, "Are there other reasons why we can't go ahead and deliver this television set to your home today?" The prospect mumbles, stalls, and says, "Well, that's more money than we want to spend."

You might paraphrase by saying, "I understand how you *feel*...$799.50 is a large sum to spend on a television set...." Then continue by saying, "Most of our customers have *felt* the same way you do before they purchased a set.

But after they carefully thought about it, they *found* that a set like this will last ten to fifteen years, and that figures out to be about a dollar a week. That's not much to pay for such a fine set as this, is it?"

Study this strategy carefully. You'll find many ways and times to use it. Here's an outline of it:

1. Listen and paraphrase the objection back to your customers.
2. Go through the Feel, Felt, Found Formula.
3. Translate the objection into a value question.

These psychological, persuasive skills work through the instinctive levels of people—not necessarily through their conscious levels. They work most effectively when you do them with sincerity—when you don't try to be manipulative with them, but when you want to help your prospects make buying decisions because they'll benefit from them.

These strategies are very powerful in neutralizing ego defenses and buyer resistance. And, it's the ego that bombs many sales!

IDENTIFY SPECIFIC OBJECTIONS— GET AGREEMENT THAT THESE ARE THE ONLY ONES

A good way to carry out this action guide, once you understand what the problem is, is to say, "If I understand the main problem, it is...(and here state the main objection)." Then once your prospects agree that you've identified the main problem or reason for not buying now, you'll want to "nail it down" and "build a fence around it."

You can do this by saying, "Other than this, is there any reason why we shouldn't go ahead now?" This keeps them from bringing out another reason after you answer the one they give you.

DISCUSS POSSIBLE SOLUTIONS— ASK PROSPECTS' OPINIONS FOR BEST ONES

Once you've isolated and identified the specific objection, you're now ready to sit down with your prospects and discuss possible solutions. Ask for their opinion for the best solution. Make this a team effort—both of you on the same side trying to come up with the best way to work things out.

Get them thinking, sharing, and discussing possible solutions. Picture yourself as a helper or counselor; a role in which you help your prospects make the best decision.

DEALING WITH PRICE OBJECTIONS

The whole sales force was lower'n a mole's navel as they came into the sales meeting that I was conducting! Faces were turned down. Chins were dragging the floor. Man, were they down! It didn't take long for them to let me know that their main competitor had started cutting prices. There was no way they'd ever make another sale. It was all lost! Beyond hope! The earth was caving in! Gloom, doom, and destruction!

I listened to them bemoan their plight. After an hour they emptied most of their despair. They were pleading for help.

"Do you have any features and product advantages that your competitors don't?" I asked.

"Oh yes," they replied.

"What are they?" I asked.

They listed several.

"Is what you're asking worth the money?" I asked.

"Oh yes," they replied.

"Then you've got no problem," I said, "and you'll see that this is true this week!"

They looked doubtful.

"Price is almost never the main consideration," I went on, pausing a moment to let my words soak in.

"Your prospects all live in homes that cost more than a lot of cheaper ones. They drive cars that are certainly not the cheapest ones they could find. They have furniture and television sets that are more expensive than some they could've bought. So price isn't their main concern! Is it?"

Then I had them all write down the three or four main benefits they could give their customers that their competition couldn't.

I instructed them to use the Feel, Felt, Found Formula and then ask, "Is the initial price your most important consideration, or for a few more dollars wouldn't you really rather have...(and mention the three benefits that their competition doesn't have)."

I sold them on the fact that initial price isn't always the most important consideration, that people really want *value!* And value is measured by length of service, amount of enjoyment, and other factors as well as the initial price. We role-played the responses. They began to feel better. The next week they came back to the sales meeting. They looked as if they could conquer the world. They'd tripled their weekly sales goals that week.

Analyze this true story and see if there's a lesson for you in it. We all get "snake bitten" about price. But it's not always the most important consideration.

Usually *value* is!

OVERCOME OBJECTIONS BY STRONGLY BELIEVING IN YOUR PRODUCT'S VALUE

When you get right down to it, nothing influences your prospects to change their minds as much as your strong, genuine belief in the value of what you're selling.

When you really believe, you'll not only communicate the right words; but you'll communicate in a much deeper, subliminal level. Your prospects will "feel" your strength and will be powerfully influenced by it.

WHEN YOU ANSWER AN OBJECTION, ALWAYS ASK A QUESTION IMMEDIATELY!

There's a very important psychological phenomenon that you can make work for you in this negotiation step. It's this: just after prospects express strong objections, their feelings will often swing to the opposite position! If you'll side-step them by using the techniques I've told you about in this chapter, then immediately ask a trial-close or a closing question, you'll often get a very favorable response.

This takes courage! But it often works! So immediately after responding to an objection, come right back and ask for action. Ask a trial-close or a close question.

TRICKS AND MANIPULATIONS

I don't believe in tricks, high pressure, or manipulation. I think professional salespeople are above that—they've found it usually doesn't work over the long haul. It usually backfires!

The strategies I've given you aren't meant to be tricks or ways to outslick your prospects.

The fact is that when people are faced with a buying decision, they need someone to help them understand the facts and make a value decision. You can't make people buy, but you can help them choose or select the best value. You can give them facts, reasons, and information.

SUMMING UP

In almost all sales transactions, a certain amount of negotiation has to occur. If we allow it, negotiation can become a battle of egos between salespeople and prospects. The salespeople always lose this battle! They can't win!

The Feel, Felt, Found Formula can be an automatic response you give whenever you meet objections, stalls, or put-offs. It's a very effective strategy in negotiation.

People's strongest emotional needs are: to be valued and understood! They're often willing to exchange their objections for our value and understanding. Remember, price isn't always the most important factor in a sale. Value usually is!

Usually when we don't successfully negotiate, it's because we didn't interview, demonstrate, or validate well. We didn't complete the prior steps.

Above all, remember that integrity negotiation is always a win-win situation.

When you let the customers have the last word, they'll often let you have their last dollar!

NEGOTIATION

Action Guides to Practice This Week

1. Ask, "Is there anything that's keeping you from buying now?"
2. Welcome objections—let prospects know that you understand how they feel.
3. Identify specific objections—get agreement that these are the only ones.
4. Discuss possible solutions—ask prospects' opinions for the best solution.

Willingham's Wisdom

There was once a low-paid saleperson named Chauveaux,
Who hadn't learned to control his own ego.
    When it came time to negotiate,
    Conflicts and arguments he'd initiate,
And time after time the sale he'd blow!

(Freak out, Freud!)

Chapter Seven

CLOSE—
How to Exchange
What You're Selling
for Your Customer's Money!

M y wife found the new car she wanted, so together we
went to buy it. The salesman was nice, at first. We
pointed out the one she wanted and asked his best price. He
figured a while, flipped through an inventory booklet,
added up some figures, and told us the price.

I offered him a lesser amount. He grimaced but finally
agreed. I told him we'd take the car. My wife was so anxious
to get it that she had the check written out very quickly.

Then the salesman told us he'd have to get the deal approved. So taking our check with him, he went into the sales manager's office. They got into a long discussion, which, I suppose, was designed to impress us.

Finally, the salesman came back and said that he'd tried to get us the best deal he could, but that he apparently figured the cost too low because the sales manager turned it down. Then he said that we'd have to pay him $100 more.

"But you gave us a price which we accepted!" I shot back.

He backpeddled a while, fumbling for words, and then visited the sales manager again.

When he came out, he had "good" news. The sales manager said he could go ahead and knock off another $50. Which, of course, meant that we'd have to pay an additional $50.

Although we wanted the car and were set to drive it home that evening, I was irritated at the snow job I had received!

I got our check back and left.

The salesman called me the next day and offered to take the amount we'd originally agreed upon, but I wouldn't accept. We bought a car just like it at another dealer for the same price we'd first agreed upon and since then, I wouldn't get within a mile of going into that dealer's showroom. Their tricky, manipulative strategy insulted and offended me. Had they been straight with me, they'd have made a sale then and probably several more later on.

It's my opinion that most people are smart enough not to fall for gimmicky closes. They often resent them. I think I see less and less of them today than in years past.

I think that today's average buyers want straight, honest dealings with salespeople. They want honest value at a fair price. They smell tricks and manipulation a mile off, and most are turned off by them. They're de-motivators.

A couple of years ago I was talking to a business owner about doing some sales training for him. He made a statement that turned me off. He said, "All good salesmen have a streak of larceny in them!" In my opinion, that's 180 degrees from the truth.

CLOSING IS SIMPLY ASKING

Emerson once wrote, "The highest price you can pay for a thing is to ask!" He's right!

For many salespeople, asking is the most difficult part of selling. This difficulty wrecks many salespeople. They do a good job of approaching, interviewing, demonstrating, validating, and negotiating. And just when everything is going *well*, and it's time to wrap up the sale, they freeze, flake, fold, or fumble.

When it comes time to close, many salespeople begin to make excuses that let their prospects off the hook. Often prospects are ready to buy and trying to buy, but the saleperson does illogical things such as saying: "Now, I don't want to pressure you!"; or, "Maybe you want more time to think about this."; or they do other weak strategies that almost block their prospects from buying.

Because of fear of rejection or other emotional reasons, salespeople get very weak when it comes time to close. Studies have shown that in up to 90 percent of all sales calls, salespeople fail to *ask* their prospects to buy. Unbelievable, isn't it? But when salespeople are trained to ask, after they've completed the prior steps of the sales system, their sales go up significantly.

YOU CAN'T CLOSE UNTIL
YOU COMPLETE THE PRIOR STEPS

My experience has led me to believe that failure to close is usually the result of not completing the prior steps of my sales system. The approach step was not handled well. Needs were not sufficiently identified or the right thing was not demonstrated. Product or service claims and facts were not validated or proved. A "win-win" situation was not negotiated.

Theoretically, when all prior steps are accomplished, a close is a natural thing to do. A natural decision that you simply ask for.

When your prospects don't buy, it doesn't necessarily mean that you didn't close well. It may mean that you bogged down long before getting to the close—that you didn't do something else well.

DON'T TRY TO CLOSE UNTIL
YOUR PROSPECT IS READY TO CLOSE

For years, I've heard the old bromide, "Close early and often!" That's about the dumbest thing I've ever heard! I don't want to ask for a closing decision until I'm pretty well assured of getting a positive response.

It's sales suicide to ask a person to buy when we're pretty sure of getting a negative response. Why? Because when people say "no" to a closing question, they've planted themselves in a firmer position. Very often when we hang in there and try to convince them, we get into an ego battle. We've forced them into a stand that's more difficult to retreat from.

In a moment I'll share with you how you can ask trial-closing questions that'll help you know when the right time to close is.

ACTION GUIDES TO PRACTICE
FOR EFFECTIVE CLOSING

Here are four action guides to help you close more effectively. These guides are designed to be practiced by you over and over until they become habits:

1. Ask trial-closing questions to get opinions and responses.
2. Give positive reinforcement.
3. Restate how benefits will outweigh costs.

4. Ask them to buy now—hold eye contact and silently wait for their answer.

ASK TRIAL-CLOSING QUESTIONS
TO GET OPINIONS AND RESPONSES

As I mentioned in another chapter, a trial-close question is one that gets an *opinion*. A close question is one that gets a *decision*.

You can begin asking trial-closing questions during your demonstration step—after you've asked enough need-development questions.

Your trial-closing questions should be pretty non-threatening when you first begin asking them. Then in your negotiation you can get more direct with them. What do I mean?

Here are several typical trial-close or opinion-getting questions. Notice how they increase in directness:

"How does this sound to you?"

"What do you think of this feature?"

"Which of these do you like best?"

"How do you feel this will answer your needs?"

"What other thoughts do you have?"

"Is this the general price range you were thinking of?"

"Other than yourself, who'll be in on the decision?"

"What other information will you need before making a decision?"

These examples will help you think of other trial-close questions that'll fit your product or service.

From the time you begin your demonstration to the point that you feel a close is appropriate, your objective is to get opinions, reactions, feelings, or feedback. Trial-close questions give you these.

You can get this information without being threatening or pushy. These types of questions get your prospects talking and you listening. It helps them sort out their own thinking and sell themselves. It impresses them that you're not just trying to cram something down their throats. It's another trust-building activity. It also gives you lots of information about where you are with your prospects.

GIVE POSITIVE REINFORCEMENT

My friend, Bill Johnson, is one terrific salesman! He sells people on investing large amounts of money with him. He's got this strange habit of nodding his head up and down everytime you say something to him. As he nods, he'll say, "Uh huh...yeah...I see"and other affirmative reinforcers.

Now everyone knows to do that when people say or give us positive responses. But Bill does it even when he gets a negative response! It doesn't seem to make any difference if people agree or disagree with him, he gives them the same positive reinforcement.

You can't argue with the guy! His low-keyed, positive reinforcement is a powerful persuader. It's dynamite in winning others to his way of thinking.

He's got a standard line that he uses instinctively when he gets a negative response. He'll nod his head up and down in approval and say, "Yeah...I know what you mean...."

He'll concede the validity of their points, and then with the tenacity of a charging rhinoceros he'll counter with, "But let me ask you this...." Then he'll ask a pointed question that helps them see the other side of the picture. He does this without the slightest hint of conflict or combativeness. He never puts his ego on the line, nor does he tromp on other people's egos.

He instinctively gives positive reinforcement to people—whether they give him positive or negative responses.

Well, let me jump back and talk more about positive reinforcement. Salespeople give positive reinforcement by:

1. Making rewarding remarks
2. Nodding and showing physical signs of approval
3. Signifying agreement—both physically and verbally

When do we give positive reinforcement? We give it each time we get responses from people—responses to our trial close and attempted-close questions. We give positive reinforcement *regardless* of whether we get positive or negative responses from people. This is powerful persuasion!

When we ask several trial-close questions and positively reinforce people's responses, they're instinctively impelled to give us back positive responses.

Without thinking—they're impelled to return positive reinforcement to us! This is a natural law! The Law of Psychological Reciprocity! That's heavy, heavy stuff!

RESTATE HOW BENEFITS WILL OUTWEIGH COSTS

Before you ask a closing question, it's a good idea to restate how the benefits of your offering will outweigh the costs to the buyer.

Gary Barton works for Corporate Systems, a firm that sells risk-management computer software systems to large Fortune 500 companies. Some of his sales involve significant outlays from companies.

Recently he sold a system to one of the largest hospital-supply manufacturers in the world. The sale involved about a $60,000 annual income to his company.

Gary had followed my sales system from start to finish. He got the decision-makers together in one meeting, including the company treasurer. He gained rapport. He interviewed, asked need-development questions, got the people involved telling him their needs. He demonstrated his systems to them. He validated by sharing how other companies had used his systems to save money. He negotiated the price.

Then it was time to close....How did he do it? Did he use tricks or pressure tactics?

No!

When he saw that they were ready to buy—when all the previous steps has been successfully completed—he restated how the benefits outweighed the costs. Then he asked a closing question.

Here's how he did it.

To pave the way for a closing question, he carefully repeated these thoughts that he'd said earlier in the presentation:

"Every day that you go without this system, it costs you money!"

"If what you're buying isn't worth at least twice what you're paying, we need to reevaluate the system!"

Then he restated the benefits. The benefits were controlling costs and having better management information.

Then he said:

"We've identified your basic needs. I've shown you how we can respond to these needs! At this point we need to get a form of authorization from you as it'll take about thirty days to get this system operational. Would you prefer to sign a contract now, or give us a letter of intent so we can go ahead and order the terminals?"

When he asked this closing question, he was sure of getting a "yes." How was he sure? Because he'd asked several trial-close questions that brought back their feelings and opinions.

"I don't use magic closes," Gary told me. "I don't have to! There's no need for it!"

He went on, "All the selling takes place back in the interview, demonstration, and validation steps. The close is just a time to wrap-up things after I've sold 'em!"

ASK THEM TO BUY NOW— HOLD EYE CONTACT AND SILENTLY WAIT FOR THEIR ANSWER

Although the selling takes place back in prior steps, there comes a time when we must *ask!* In my opinion, the time to ask is when we think we'll get a positive response.

There are several ways of asking. Let's think about only three. These will be used most of the time and can be adapted to different situations.

The three ways to ask are:

1. The assumptive close
2. The either-or close
3. The simply-ask close

THE ASSUMPTIVE-CLOSE QUESTION

Gary Barton's close was both assumptive and either-or. He assumed they were going to go ahead when he asked them which way they wanted to make a commitment.

Gene Klein, Jr., uses the assumptive close to sell fire and burglar-alarm systems to homeowners and businesses. First, he identifies his prospect's needs, lays out the recommended system, validates it, and presents the price.

He asks these trial-close questions. Notice what information they bring back:

"Will this protect all the areas you want protected?" he'll ask. "Will this help you feel safer and more secure from surprise burglars?" "Will this help you feel better knowing that your irreplaceable antiques, jewelry (or whatever they have) will be safer?"

After asking and getting affirmative responses to these trial-close questions, he knows that it's time to close. He's been filling out a contract all along. He looks it over again and asks, "Is there anything else we should include in your system before we finalize the contract?"

Very often there is something else they want to include. This is all right with him. But if they don't want anything else, he'll mark an "X" on the contract and ask them to sign it.

He's learned that it's a very good way to wrap things up.

How can you use the assumptive close in your selling? How can you ask, "In addition to the things I've proposed, what else needs to be included before we wrap things up?"

THE EITHER-OR CLOSE

The either-or close simply gives a prospect a choice between two alternatives, or a choice between secondary options.

When I was in college, a couple of hundred years ago, I worked part-time for an office-supply company. The first thing people saw when entering the store was a glass showcase containing Sheaffer and Parker fountain pens and desk sets. Few people use fountain pens anymore, but then everyone did.

I learned when demonstrating them to keep no more than two different ones out on top of the case at one time. When customers looked at one they didn't like, I'd put it back in the case before taking another out. Finally, if they were serious about buying, the choice would always be between the two remaining ones.

An easy closing question was, "Which of these do you like the best?" If they responded positively, I'd put the other pen set back in the case, close the door, hand them the one they chose, and proceed to write out a sales slip. I didn't ask them if they wanted to buy one; I asked them which they liked the best. This is a simple example of the either-or close.

Many insurance salespeople use the either-or close with effectiveness. In presenting a policy, they'll attempt a close by asking, "Should we include the family-income rider?" "Shall we include the waiver of premium feature?"

You might find it profitable to write out some either-or questions that you can quickly recall for a close. You may find that using them gives you a powerful closing tool. They'll help you get closing decisions without being heavy-handed or combative.

THE SIMPLY-ASK CLOSE

Often, after you've restated the benefits your prospects will receive, it's appropriate to simply ask them to buy.

You ask them to make a decision!

The manner in which you ask it depends on the situation, your personality, your prospect's personality, and the rapport you have.

Use the appropriate words that ask your prospects to make a decision.

RECOGNIZE YOUR PROSPECT'S FEAR OF MAKING A DECISION

I was visiting with the marketing director of a firm about conducting a two-day annual sales conference for his salespeople.

We spent a half-day discussing his needs. I learned as much as I could about the service his firm marketed: what its features, advantages, and benefits were; what his salespeople weren't doing that he wanted them to do.

Everything seemed to be acceptable to him. I asked him what other questions he had or what other information he needed to give me.

He said that everything had been discussed pretty well.

"Then may I go ahead and schedule these dates?" I asked him.

He stalled me, saying he wanted to think about it for a few days. As he said this, I nodded up and down and said, "I appreciate your desire to make the right decision."

I went on, "If you're not ready to firm this up now, there must be some more information or references you need. Is this true?"

"Oh, no!" he replied. "I think you'll do a good job."

"I assure you I will," I said. "Should I go ahead and hold these dates and then check back with you in a couple of days for final confirmation?"

"Yeah, that'll be fine," he answered, relaxing a bit.

I smiled and nodded and let him know that this was all right. I folded my briefcase and leaned back for a few moments of closing conversation.

"You run a big risk, don't you, when you book a speaker?" I asked him.

"Yeah, I sure do."

"I can understand that," I said. "If a speaker bombs, it's your head, isn't it?"

"Yeah," he grinned. "The one we had last year bombed! The president made it quite clear that that isn't to happen again!"

"I understand," I said.

He relaxed a bit more. We chatted for a few minutes about an upcoming football game. Then out of the clear blue sky he said, "Oh, I don't see any reason for you to call me back. Just go ahead and firm up those dates. I know you'll do a good job!" When he said that, I thanked him and left.

I'm sure that taking the pressure off him helped him make the decision.

He was afraid that he'd have his head on the chopping block again if I didn't do well. And at the final decision point, that fear reared up. If I had pressed him for a decision before I dealt with his fear, I may have blown the whole sale.

So, my point is—always recognize your prospects' potential fear of making a final decision when you close. Try to neutralize their fear before you ask direct-closing questions.

SUMMING UP

Closing isn't tricks, manipulation, or using gimmicks. It isn't outsmarting your prospects. It's not faking them into buying, or using verbal strategies that they can't cope with.

Closing is simply asking the prospect to buy after you've completed the prior steps of:

Approach
Interview

Demonstrate

Validate

Negotiate

Closing is simply asking. Emerson wrote, "The highest price you can pay for a thing is to ask!"

Don't try to close until the prospect is ready to close? How do you know when he or she is ready? You know by asking trial-close questions. A trial-close question is one that asks for an *opinion!* A closing question is one that calls for a *decision!*

Negative-opinion responses are easy to deal with. *Negative-decision* responses are difficult to deal with because they cause a prospect to take a stand that might be difficult to change. They also draw both of you into combat when you try to change his or her mind.

Learn to give positive reinforcement—when you get a positive response *and* when you get a negative response.

There comes the time in every sale to take action and ask for a decision. Here are three ways to ask:

1. The assumptive close

2. The either-or close

3. The simply-ask close

Anticipate your prospect's fear of making a final decision. This fear almost always comes up. Take time to neutralize it before you ask the final direct-close question.

Follow these ideas. Practice them until they become habits. They'll help you exchange what you're selling for your customer's money!

CLOSING

Action Guides to Practice This Week

1. Ask trial-closing questions to get opinions.
2. Give positive reinforcement.
3. Restate how benefits will outweigh costs.
4. Ask them to buy now—hold eye contact and silently wait for their answer.

Willingham's Wisdom

There was once an undernourished salesperson named Levi,
Who was too timid to *ask* his prospects to buy!
    When it came time to close,
    Everything within him froze,
Until he finally got up the *courage* to try!

                (Way to go, Thoreau!)

Chapter Eight

How to Condition Your Mind to Receive Fatter Commission Checks!

This chapter will be quick and brief! If you're ready, and are truly searching for greater sales success, you'll find in this chapter the rocket fuel to launch yourself into new worlds of achievement, self-esteem, and earnings.

I'm going to share with you a mind-conditioning process that a very wealthy salesman told me had a large part in helping him accumulate several hundred-million dollars!

The salesman to whom I'm referring is W. Clement Stone, a man who understands the truth that all thought and action begin in the subconscious mind. Understanding this truth can be especially rewarding for salespeople like you and me.

The truth is that each of us has a subconscious belief system—formed by our responses to all our past experiences. This belief system, or self-image, or mental paradigm controls all our actions, feelings, behavior, and abilities! We always act consistently with what we *believe* to be true about ourselves! This means that we unconsciously engineer success or failure—depending on whether our self-image is positive or negative.

Stop a moment and chew around on that concept! It's a blockbuster!

It explains why some salespeople do well and enjoy a better-than-average lifestyle, and why others do poorly and barely scrounge by.

OUR SUCCESS IN SELLING IS CONSISTENT WITH OUR BELIEF SYSTEM

I see this law of success all the time in sales-training seminars and courses.

Not long ago, I conducted a seminar for a company that had twenty salespeople. The sales manager gave me a written evaluation and earnings of each person prior to my going to conduct the seminar. I was very impressed with the high incomes that most earned.

The sales manager also told me that there was one salesman who wasn't performing up to his potential, and there was a question as to whether he'd be able to keep his job. He said the man should be his best sales performer but instead was his weakest.

It was eerie, but when I began the seminar, I spotted this man instantly! He was the only one in the room with his arms folded. His mind was a million miles away, and he obviously resented being there.

Ironically, he was the sharpest-looking person in the whole room. He was very athletic-looking and handsome. He knew how to put colors together and dress well. His appearance was very impressive.

If you'd stood all the salesmen up and let ten people choose the one who was most likely to succeed, probably everyone would have chosen him. He was that sharp-looking!

In the morning session he acted detached, bored, and suspicious, and hardly participated in group discussions. At lunch I made it a point to sit by him and try to talk to him. He finally warmed up a bit but still displayed a suspicious, superior attitude. I found out that he'd been in training a few years earlier for the Olympic Decathlon. He talked about it for a minute or so then quickly changed the subject.

Then on the evening of the second day, at a reception, I spotted him and tried to strike up some conversation with him.

I asked him to tell me more about his Olympic experience. It took a few minutes, but he began to open up and talk. He told me that he'd been second or third in the running for the Decathlon until he injured himself and had to drop out of competition.

"I suppose you were really crushed?" I asked him.

He opened up and talked about that for a few minutes, how it had been his most important goal. Obviously, he'd not replaced it with new, exciting goals. I had the feeling that he thought his life was behind him. That nothing else would ever come along as exciting as the Olympics. We talked for twenty to thirty minutes. I hoped that I'd helped him, but seriously doubted that I had.

Then a few weeks later, he either quit his job or was replaced. I suspected that deep down he saw himself as a loser who felt robbed and cheated and expected it to happen again. Or, maybe, coming from the recognition of an Olympic participant to a sales job was a real downer!

Whatever the real reasons, his self-image, or belief system, kept his real talents and abilities well locked up.

Performing on his job wasn't consistent with his belief system.

The same principle works in reverse for high performers. Their actions, feelings, behavior, and abilities are consistent with what they believe to be true about themselves. They mentally see themselves as achievers.

EXPANDING YOUR BELIEF SYSTEM

Since you desire more success, achievement, and the good things of life, your next question probably is, "Well, how do I strengthen my belief system so my performance will automatically increase?" I'm glad you asked because that's what the balance of this chapter is about!

What I'll present to you is a system to help you increase your performance!

You'll think of many other ways to benefit from the system I'll share with you.

SUGGESTION, SELF-SUGGESTION, AUTO-SUGGESTION

To understand the dynamic process that I'll share with you, it's important to understand three concepts. They are: "suggestion," "self-suggestion," and "auto-suggestion." In the context that I'll use them, here are definitions of these three concepts.

A *suggestion* is anything that comes into your consciousness and registers an impact upon you. The suggestion may be in the form of words, pictures, or other sensory inputs. You're being subjected to suggestions all the time—through television, newspapers, radio, and other ways.

Self-suggestion is the act of consciously suggesting thoughts to yourself through words you say. When you say thoughts to yourself repeatedly, over a period of time you'll eventually come to *believe* or *accept* these thoughts as fact.

Understanding this law of the mind can give you a clue to changing the way you think. For instance, if you want to develop a new thought-pattern, belief, or value, you can use *self-suggestion* by consciously repeating the desired attitude fifty times in the morning and fifty times in the evening.

Then, if you'll keep this up for at least three to four weeks, you'll begin to subconsciously "believe" what you've suggested. At this point, your subconscious has "bought" the idea or thought. Your subconscious will then influence your actions and keep them consistent with your inner beliefs.

Auto-suggestion is when your subconscious has accepted an idea or thought. It *automatically* flashes thoughts to your consciousness when you need them.

Let me give you an example. Early in my adult life, I discovered that I thoroughly enjoyed putting things off. Whenever I saw something that needed to be done, I'd put it off. It got me into a lot of trouble.

Then I read Napoleon Hill and W. Clement Stone's book, *Success Through a Positive Mental Attitude*. It introduced me to the process I'm sharing with you. So, fifty times in the morning and fifty times in the evening, I began saying to myself, "When I see something that needs to be done, I do it!" "When I see something that needs to be done, I do it!"

After a few weeks of saying this to myself each day, a strange thing began happening. Everytime I saw something that needed to be done, this thought would *automatically* flash from my subconscious to my conscious mind, "When you see something that needs to be done, you do it!" Then I'd find myself responding with action—doing the thing that needed to be done.

OK, so now you understand "suggestion," "self-suggestion," and "auto-suggestion." Now, let me give you the system.

CONDITIONING YOUR MIND BY SELF-SUGGESTION

Here are six suggestions that can help you in your sales career. They'll help you strengthen yourself in these six areas:

1. Time management
2. Closing ability
3. Making quality calls
4. Attracting prosperity
5. Seeing yourself as a respected professional
6. Overcoming fear of rejection

Here are the six suggestions. I want you to copy each one on a separate index card:

"I realize that time is my most valuable resource—so I carefully use it on result-producing activities!"

"My closing ratio gets higher and higher, because the more I ask, the more I sell!"

"The more quality calls I make—the more income dollars I earn!"

"I attract prosperity by associating with prosperous people!"

"I am a professional, respected person—capable of earning a professional, respected income!"

"I enjoy calling on people—people enjoy my calling on them!"

HOW TO PUT THESE SUGGESTIONS INTO A SYSTEM THAT'LL WORK FOR YOU

Now, in order to make these work for you, you'll need to perform the following system or process:

1. Write these six suggestions on six 3-by-5 cards.
2. Put a rubber band around them and carry them with you each day.
3. Begin with, "I enjoy calling on people—people enjoy my calling on them!"

   a. Say it to yourself fifty times each morning
      and fifty times each evening.
   b. Do it for six days in a row.
4. The next week flip the card to the back and go
   through the same process for the next suggestion.

Then when you've gone six weeks, begin again with the first suggestion. Do it another six weeks. Then another. That's it! That's all you have to do.

In time, and it'll take several weeks, you'll begin to be aware of changes in the way you think and respond to people. Your confidence will grow; you will have less call-reluctance. Your belief system will be expanded—you'll see yourself as a higher paid saleperson. Your self-image will grow—you'll feel more professional. Your fears will diminish.

Your sales achievements will increase! They'll increase consistently with your expanded belief system.

Now, let me be negative for a moment and say that you'll have to exercise some mental discipline in order to stick with this process long enough to benefit from it. I know, because I give this to many people at seminars. Later, I find that some *do* it and benefit greatly. Others think it's "hokey" and never do it. Others start it but drop it in a few days.

But I'll look you straight in your right eyeball and make a promise to you! I promise you that this'll work for you if you'll work it!

Do it day in and day out. At first, don't logically assess its validity. Just do it. Then, after a month or two, stop and assess it and see if you aren't noticing results. Then keep on for a year. Yes, a whole year! And every time you're tempted to cheat, visualize that I'm watching you! Then at the end of the first year, send me 10% of your earnings' increase! (I'm just kidding—so don't flood me with money!)

SUMMING UP

Read this chapter several times. Write out your cards and carry them with you each day. Say the suggestion to yourself, out loud, fifty times in the morning and fifty times in the evening. Do this for six days in a row. Then the next week go to the second card. Do it for a week. After the sixth week, begin again. Repeat it several times.

This process will change and positively increase your self-beliefs. *Then, as you believe more, you'll produce more,* automatically!

This system of mind conditioning might just put more money in your pockets than anything else you've ever done! This chapter can be a blockbuster for you. It can be mental dynamite; income magic; the key to your personal growth; and the point from which your success skyrockets!

Follow these suggestions to the letter, and I'll promise you that you'll condition your mind to receive fatter commission checks!

Willingham's Wisdom

There was once a negative salesperson named Ravenelli,
Whose self-image was as low as a snake's belly!
   Then he began saying a daily self-suggestion,
   Until he discovered beyond any question,
That his success could be sweet and not smelly!

(A savvy saying, 'eh, Solomon?)

Chapter Nine

How to Squeeze
More Money
Out of Your Time

Here are some ways I've observed that salespeople spend their time. Many salespeople tend to cram more time into their calls, rather than cramming more calls into their time! Many salespeople spend 80 percent of their time getting 20 percent of their sales—they spend 20 percent of their time getting 80 percent of their sales! This means that 20 percent of their time is used with maximum productivity.

Many salespeople confuse activity for productivity! They confuse busy-ness for business! Why? Well, mainly for these reasons:

1. Call reluctance, and mental inertia
2. Shuffling papers, or doing unimportant details
3. Calling on unqualified prospects
4. Lack of planning and organization

There are other reasons, but I've observed these to be the most destructive ones.

YOU HAVE TO WANT TO USE YOUR TIME BETTER BEFORE YOU WILL!

This is true! You have to want to use your time better before you will. You also must be willing to put up with some pain! For me, the discipline of overcoming poor time management was painful, at first. But then, most discipline is, isn't it? Painful at first, but rewarding later.

So, let me say that if you're willing to endure some pain of discipline, this chapter can help you enjoy some new levels of confidence, time efficiency, and income. And if you're like me, you have to work on this discipline constantly.

Only you can decide whether the rewards will outweigh the discipline.

"I REALIZE THAT TIME IS MY MOST VALUABLE RESOURCE— SO I CAREFULLY USE IT ON RESULT-PRODUCING ACTIVITIES!"

I found that this self-suggestion, that I shared with you in the last chapter, needed to be programmed into my mental computer *as a value* before I was motivated to practice effective time-management techniques.

Deep down, I had to *want* to manage my time better. Unless I wanted to, I wouldn't manage my time well.

By the way, how are you doing on your self-suggestions? Have you been saying one to yourself fifty times in the morning and fifty times in the evening, for a week? Salespeople who do the above suggestion tell me that in three or four weeks they suddenly find themselves *wanting* to make an extra call in the afternoon.

They find themselves wanting to do routine paperwork before and after selling hours. They find themselves mentally sifting for better prospects. They look for ways to maximize their efficiency.

You see, the *inner value, motive,* or *desire* is the cause that produces the effects of planning and discipline. Effective time management is an effect. An effect!

It's caused first by desire, and then by planning, by organization, and by developing proper habits! All the advice, systems, strategies, or information on time management will fail, if the desire, motive, or inner value isn't firmly established within us. I want to be tough-minded about this! I don't want us to kid ourselves! I want us to have the courage to face the truth!

You can read this chapter a dozen times, but before you'll *benefit* from it you must honestly want:

1. To get more selling done in less time
2. To *follow* the system or strategy

First, program this value into your subconscious, "I realize that time is my most valuable resource—so I carefully use it on result-producing activities!" Say this to yourself fifty times in the morning and fifty times in the evening for a week. Then come back to this chapter and perform the system.

A SYSTEM FOR MORE EFFECTIVE
TIME MANAGEMENT

Here's a four-step system for squeezing more money out of your time:

1. Plan
2. Prioritize
3. Plod
4. Pay

PLAN

Your plan should include these two elements:

1. A sales objective
2. A strategy for reaching this objective

To plan, define sales objectives for this next year, six months, three months, one month. Obviously the objectives would account for seasonal ups and downs, vacations, holidays, and other factors. Plot these on a calendar.

Once these long-range volume goals are set, break them down into monthly goals and weekly goals. Then ask yourself, "What am I going to do each day to reach my objectives?"

Each day's sales calls and activities should be geared to reaching well-defined weekly, monthly, and yearly goals.

It's here that a day or two taken from your selling and invested in planning can pay huge dividends. Sometime before the end of this month, take a day or so and set your sales-volume goals for the balance of your fiscal or calendar year. Then, to the best of your ability, realistically break your sales goals down into monthly and weekly objectives—remembering seasonal fluctuations and other factors.

PRIORITIZE

In your planning, you defined your long-range and monthly objectives. Then, each Friday or Saturday, write down your sales goals for the next week. Once you've defined the volume goal, list the activities or calls you'll need to make. Out beside each call, write the expected results of the call. Then prioritize them—number them in order of their result-producing importance.

PLOD

Once your plans and priorities are set, it's time to go to work! Set aside minimal calling times each day. Begin at a certain time and quit at a certain time. Allow no interferences. Work like crazy during these hours! Ignite your afterburners, and break the sound barrier!

Remember that work is work! Yes, you can make some of it fun. Yes, you can enjoy it. But when you get right down to it, work is work!

But as achievers, it's something that you and I are willing to commit to in order to reach our goals. Right? So, roll up your sleeves and go to work! Don't allow unproductive influences to mess up your work hours! Work your plan!

PAY

One of the secrets of motivation is to reward yourself after you've worked hard. Reward yourself daily, weekly, monthly, and annually! In chapter one I wrote about setting motivational goals—goals that you'll give yourself when you reach your sales-volume goals. It's psychological dynamite!

What kind of daily rewards can you give yourself? How about such things as a dinner out, or a show or movie? Buy a new book. Reward yourself with an hour just to sit on your patio and listen to the birds chirp. Reserve a quiet time in the evening. Go to a ball game. Have a special visit with friends. Do whatever you'd enjoy doing at the end of that day that gives you something to look forward to.

RECAP OF THE SYSTEM

Here's an outline summary of the system I've just given you:

1. Plan
    A. Write out long-range sales-volume goals.
    B. Break them down into monthly and weekly volume goals.
    C. Write out daily activities and calls.
2. Prioritize
    A. Write out the expected result beside each daily activity or call.
    B. Number activities in order of result-producing importance.
3. Plod
    A. Begin at a certain time each day—allow no interferences.
    B. Commit yourself to minimal selling hours and work your prioritized plan.
4. Pay
    A. Give yourself daily, weekly, and monthly rewards for working your plan.
    B. Plan rewards that you'll look forward to enjoying.

Well, there you have it—a time-management system to follow.

No magic about it.

You've seen similar ones before. But big payoffs come from habitually practicing the system.

THE PURPOSE OF THIS CHAPTER

I've purposely kept this chapter very short! Why? Well, because I want to emphasize that good time management is following a simple, logical, organized system. The objective is to *do* it, not just *know* it.

The important questions are: "How can you make this system work for you?" and, "When will you begin?"

SUMMING UP

By following the system I've outlined in this chapter, you can reverse the 80-20 rule! Theoretically, if you've been spending 20 percent of your time getting 80 percent of your business, you can possibly quadruple your sales by using 100 percent of your time in total effectiveness.

Although total-time usage may be a goal you never fully reach, the striving for it will help you significantly.

Keep saying to yourself over and over, "I realize that time is my most valuable resource—so I carefully use it on result-producing activities!"

Commit yourself to spending a minimal number of hours making productive calls each day.

See how many calls you can cram into your time, rather than how much time you can cram into your calls!

Don't confuse activity for productivity! Don't confuse busy-ness for business!

As you do these things, you'll squeeze more money out of your time!

Willingham's Wisdom

There was once an emaciated salesperson named
   Cappaletti,
Who frittered away time as if it were confetti!
     But when his time he finally organized,
     And calls and activities he prioritized,
As he worked his plan, many sales records did he setti!

                       (Whatcha' think of these, Socrates?)

Chapter Ten

How to Get Your Customers Saying, "I'm Going to Buy from You Because I Like You and Trust You!"

In the height of his career, Elmer Leterman sold more life insurance than anyone else ever had! Years ago, when it was rare for an agent to sell a million dollars a year, Elmer sold up to $250,000,000 each year. Incredible!

How did he do this?

I asked him this question as I was having lunch with him one Saturday at the Plaza Hotel in New York.

"I don't sell life insurance," he replied, "I make friends!"

He went on to tell me that he spent most of his time getting to know people and developing relationships.

How did he do it?

Each weekday he had a table reserved at the Four Seasons Restaurant. He'd invite a handful of people to be his guests. He invited people from all walks of life: sports figures, business people, writers, celebrities—all kinds.

At the luncheons, they'd get to know each other; and what each other did. Never did he try to sell anything to the people. His only purpose was to make friends and develop relationships.

Our conversation took place in the early '70's. Elmer told me that his luncheon expense for the past year was $18,000. He also kept a running diary of people who were traveling abroad or to Hawaii. Knowing people everywhere, he'd call someone at the destination point and ask her or him to meet his friends and make sure they got settled into their hotels. He'd send out plaques and momentos to hundreds of people whom he'd met. He did these things without sticking out his hand and asking people to buy insurance from him. His purpose in helping the people wasn't to sell them, it was to develop relationships.

"I don't even carry a rate book or policy information," he explained to me.

But he sold lots of insurance! Why? Because people *wanted* to buy from him! That's the way it is when we build trust relationships with people.

Well, you may not be able to afford $18,000 for luncheons, but that's not the point. What can you do in your environment to develop relationships?

CUSTOMERS BUY FROM US WHEN THEY TRUST US!

In a seminar I recently conducted, a man raised his hand and asked a question that I almost always get. He asked, "What do you do when you're calling on a purchasing agent, and you're selling the same thing for the same price that six other salespeople are selling?"

I could tell from the nods of at least one-third of the participants that they had the same problem.

"If six other people can supply the same quality products or service at the same price, then what becomes the key factor in outselling the competition?" I rephrased his question. "Is that what you're asking?"

"Yeah," he replied.

"How many of you sell the same things that other salespeople sell?" I asked.

Several raised their hands.

"When you outsell your competitors, what's the reason you do?"

Various responses and ideas were shared by the people. Most could be summed up in one sentence: the buyers trusted them, wanted to buy from them, felt more comfortable buying from them.

"Then what did you do that caused them to trust you and want to buy from you?" I asked.

Slowly their responses surfaced.

"They know that I'll take care of them!" "They like our delivery time!" "They know our terms and know that the billing won't get messed up!" "We play golf together!" "I constantly keep my customers updated on new information and technology!" "It took me a long time to crack some accounts, but when I did, they stuck with me!" "They know that when they buy from me that they get me in the process!" "They know that if there's a problem that I'll straighten it out quickly!" These were some of the responses I got to my question, "What do you do that causes your customers to want to buy from you?"

Now, stop a moment and analyze these responses. Ask yourself what they're really saying. Ask yourself, "What causes me to develop strong trust relationships with my customers?"

WHAT CAUSES US TO DEVELOP
STRONG TRUST RELATIONSHIPS?

For five years after I got out of college, I sold office supplies and equipment. I soon became an outside sales-man—calling on established customers weekly, biweekly, or monthly. I was on straight commission—the more I sold, the more I earned. So, I had a high desire to sell more.

Also, because I was sensitive and had a high fear of rejection, I wanted deeply for my customers to like me. And to want to see me coming around.

I quickly found that people love to help young people who really want to learn. I found that instead of trying to impress people, I could get them to like me more by asking them for advice.

Let me give you a couple of examples.

When I first called on John Ketler, he was abrupt and rude to me. He was the manager of a savings and loan company and controlled the purchasing for several other companies as well.

For months, I got nowhere with him.

But one day a year or so later, I was considering a small property transaction. I didn't feel confident about making a decision. So I called Mr. Ketler.

"Mr. Ketler, this is Ron Willingham...."

"We don't want anything," he replied very curtly.

"But, sir, I'm not trying...."

"I said I don't want anything today!" he sternly shot back.

"Sir, you don't understand, I'm not trying to sell you anything."

"You're not?"

"No."

"Then what do you want?"

"I want to stop by and get some advice from you."

"What?"

"Advice. I want some advice from you."

"About what?"

"Some property."

"Property?"

"Yes, sir."

"Well, come on by here!" he said, warming up with his words.

So I went by, told him what I was thinking, and asked his advice. He relaxed, smiled, leaned back, took out a long cigar and lit it, and for an hour gave me some very good advice. As he did, I could tell he liked me. Actually, I think he noticed me for the first time in the year I'd been calling on him. After that, we became good friends. He liked me and I liked him.

I showed him that I was an extra-mile person by making sure deliveries got out to him promptly. I took new product ideas to him. I helped organize some filing systems for one of his companies—that took quite a bit of my time and put very little money in my pocket. Soon, he was calling me to stop by and see him. He'd even call me at home at nights, occasionally, just to visit. When he purchased large furniture items, he'd call me. We developed a good relationship. He liked me and trusted me.

I remember calling on another man—an office manager for a dairy. He was gruff, demanding, and surly. He always acted as if someone had substituted vinegar for his morning orange juice.

Nothing pleased him. Everything was always wrong. He gave our delivery people fits as well as myself!

One day as I was calling on him, he got irritated with something and said, "You're the worst salesman in the whole world!"

I didn't say it to him, but I thought to myself, "No that would be too much of a coincidence!"

"I am?" I meekly replied.

"Yes! You don't know anything about selling! I don't see how you even make a living!"

Frankly, I wanted to punch the old grouch's lights out! But instead I said, "Well, why don't you tell me how I can become a better one."

He gladly accepted my invitation. So for over a half-hour, he gave me a customized lesson in salesmanship. I listened! Obviously, due to his sensitivity and finesse at building people up, I had some question as to the value of his advice. But, I listened!

When he finished, I thanked him, mentioned a couple of his points that I could certainly use, and thanked him again for having an interest in me. He beamed as if he'd just been awarded the Nobel Prize for Wisdom!

From then on, we had a new relationship. From time to time, I'd remind him of an idea he'd given me and how I was trying to use it.

I became "his" salesman. None of my competitors had a chance with him. He chewed them up and spit them out.

He went to another job. I'd never sold his new company a dime's worth of anything. After he got there, I sold them all their supplies. He delighted in telling people on his new job how he'd taught me all I knew!

I liked him and he liked me! We developed a trust relationship that lasted until I left that job and opened my own retail-furniture store.

ASK AN INFLUENTIAL PERSON TO HELP YOU!

In his autobiography, Benjamin Franklin tells about winning a deeply entrenched enemy to be his friend. The man had a certain rare book that Franklin wanted to read. He sent the man a note asking if he might have loan of the book for a few days—mentioning how he admired the book and how anxious he was to read it. Immediately, the man had the book delivered to Franklin. With the book as a common interest, the man's bitterness toward Franklin dissolved.

The same principle applies today. If you want to win people, ask for their help, for their advice, or for their counsel. The wisest, wealthiest person in town has time to share his or her wisdom with you if you sincerely want to learn!

CREATE NEW PROFITS FOR YOUR CUSTOMERS!

Another way to deepen relationships is to let your customers know that your objective is to help increase their profits. That bit of marketing philosophy will set you apart from most of your competitors! Get to know their business. Keep analyzing their needs.

Once, I consulted with a marketing company. Mainly, I did training seminars and sales-training sessions for them. The company sold computer software, had a sharp sales group, and was on the cutting edge of serving a new, sophisticated market. After working with them, I saw that they needed more sales-management controls. So I designed a simple sales-management system for them—on my own time.

I shared it with their president, Guyon Saunders, and he got excited. He took it, made it fit their needs in more specific ways, and implemented it. He later told me that my giving him the system was worth my whole year's consulting fee—if I did nothing else for them. I appreciated his saying that. While we've not discussed it any more, I can see how my doing that deepened our relationship.

That managment tool is creating more profits for his company. As a result, I'm more valuable to them.

BE SENSITIVE TO YOUR
CUSTOMER'S PERSONAL NEEDS!

When I sold office supplies and equipment, I found that after a customer trusted me, he or she'd often confide in me about personal problems and frustrations. I became a professional listener. I didn't have to tell my customers that they could trust my confidentiality. They just seemed to know that they could.

Years later, I found that as a sales trainer and consultant, I owed it to my clients to support them personally. I let them know that.

Once I conducted a seminar for a firm and at the end of the first day, the company vice-president, who'd hired me, came up to me and said, "I know you're tired so you and I will go out to dinner by ourselves." That was fine with me because I'd been burning high-octane fuel all day. During dinner, he mentioned that his son was having some marital problems. He asked several questions. I asked him several questions. We talked about his son's situation.

A few days later, he called me. "When will you be back through here?"

I told him.

"If you'll plan to spend a couple of hours, I'll pick you up at the airport and buy you lunch."

"Sounds good to me," I replied.

He picked me up. We'd no sooner driven off when he said, "You remember I was talking to you about my son?"

"Yes, I remember."

"Well, it wasn't my son! It was me!"

Then for two or three hours, he poured out his troubles to me. Troubles that he couldn't afford to pour out to anyone in his company hierarchy.

I listened and supported him. He trusted me. We became good friends. He gave me a lot more business. He knows that I care about him and that it's not just because of the business he gives me. He knows it's more genuine than that.

Many of my clients have children. They're concerned about their children's self-esteem. When they talk to me about this, I'll often send them some cassettes of a course called *Celebration* I wrote for pre-teen children. It's designed to help build children's self-esteem, help them deal with anger, solve problems creatively, and get along better in school and with other kids. By being interested in their children, I develop stronger relationships with them. It helps my business. But that's not the only reason I do it.

TRUST RELATIONSHIPS OFTEN TAKE TIME

When I share these things with salespeople in seminars, especially younger salespeople, they often seem disappointed and frustrated. "But these things take time!" someone often says.

Yes, they do. Trust relationships take time.

Trust relationships often escape and elude salespeople because they're interested in immediate gratification or instant magic miracles. And, too, their commitment to a job is temporary—depending on whether they can make a quick score or not. So they never reach a professional selling level. A "here today—gone tomorrow"-commitment level rarely breeds trust and customer confidence.

I find too many salespeople today saying, "I'll give this job a try and see if I can make some money. If not, I'll look for something else!"

But the pros who make it, find a product, service, or field they can get emotionally involved in. They say, "I'm making a commitment to this. I'll learn and pay my dues and see it through until I'm successful!"

The difference is in commitment and purpose. Well, admittedly, this sounds a bit preachy. But I believe it's the truth.

YOU ARE WHAT YOU COMMUNICATE!

The wise man Emerson gave us many profound thoughts. Rewarding indeed is the time spent chewing and digesting such of his classics as "Compensation," "Self-Reliance," and "Spiritual Laws."

He writes in "Spiritual Laws":

"Human character evermore publishes itself. The most fugitive deed and word, the mere air of doing a thing, the intimated purpose, expresses character. If you act you show character; if you sit still, if you sleep, you show it."

In another paragraph he writes:

"A man passes for what he's worth. What he is engraves itself on his face, on his form, on his fortunes, in letters of light. Concealment avails him nothing, boasting nothing."

Yes, "What we are speaks so loudly that people cannot hear what we say!" What's this got to do with success in selling? Everything.

Our values—what we believe and what guides our actions—are silent communications to our customers. They communicate what we are! We pass for what we are!

SUMMING UP

Enduring success in selling is enhanced as we develop trust relationships with our customers. They buy us as well as what we're selling.

What ideas did you get from reading this chapter? How do you see yourself profiled on the grid of these thoughts? What can you do to develop stronger relationships with your customers, clients, or prospects? How can you add profit to the bottom line of their companies? How can you personally support them as individuals?

How can you get them helping you? Giving advice to you? Recommending you to others?

How can you move beyond mere theory and intellectual assessment of what I've written and apply the concepts?

When will you begin? With whom?

Yes, you communicate what you are! We all publish our values and character to our customers in our every word, deed, and action! And what we *are* determines what we'll *be* with them! What we are determines whether they'll say, "I'm going to buy from you because I like you and trust you!"

Willingham's Wisdom

There was once a loud-mouthed salesperson named
  Leone,
Whom most people considered to be a big phony.
    But he discovered that to be successful he must,
    Become a person his customers can trust,
Instead of feeding them a big line of baloney!

                (No longer in the dark, Plutarch?)

Chapter Eleven

How to Grit Your Teeth and Stomp a Mudhole in Your Biggest Enemy—FEAR!

Several years ago, a veteran life insurance sales manager told me this little quip that I've thought about many times. He said, "Most young life insurance agents quickly learn how to deal with call-reluctance. They *quit* making calls!"

In my opinion, he explained why a large percent of all salespeople don't reach their goals. Fear! They suffer from; fear of rejection, fear of the unknown, fear of failure, fear of poverty, and fear of success! (Yes, fear of success!)

Probably no one is bombarded with more negative feedback than salespeople. If you're average, you probably get at least five times as many "nos" as "yeses."

Unless you're pretty well reinforced from within, these responses can unconsciously torpedo you. Fear can cause you to dread calling on people. After a few times of getting your nose busted and bloody, you may get reluctant to expose your psyche to more pain. So you quit!

I've seen this happen again and again.

In many types of selling, such as straight commission, the fear of the unknown can paralyze people. It's the fear of failure, the fear of poverty. "What happens if I don't make it?" plagues people's productivity. It negatively neutralizes them.

I've also known salepeople who even fear success! I've seen them subconsciously engineer failure so their friends or spouses would still feel comfortable with them, so they'd be consistent with negative self-beliefs, or for religious or cultural reasons! "God loves the poor!" they seem to believe, "and if I stay poor, God will keep loving me!"

Well, I don't want to spend too much time identifying fear. If you've sold, you already know what it is, and how it can rip out your emotional vitals.

My purpose is to talk about some positive strategies that'll help you with some real, workable, rubber-meets-the-road, confidence-building solutions.

My objective is to help you see yourself as a capable professional; a person of integrity; someone who adds value to other people's lives; who gives more than he takes; who honestly believes in what he's selling as a product or service of integrity; who is a value generator.

Then I want to share with you how you can enjoy tremendous emotional support by structuring a success-support system, and how you can put together a synergistic power station from which you can receive millions of kilowatts of energy, support, and confidence.

Sound as if I'm promising a lot for one single chapter? Well, plug in and plow through the next few pages because

I'm going to share some strategies that can swell your selling success.

So don't get in too big of a hurry! Slow down, meditate, question, relate, and see what you can apply.

NEED FOR COMMITMENT

What I'm about to say may sound as if I'm jumping on a soapbox and preaching to you. Maybe I am! It's been my observation that professional salespeople who enjoy sustained, long-range success share a couple of things in common:

1. They chose their field because it offers more rewards than just making money.
2. They commit their lives to it.

What's this got to do with dealing with fear? Everything!

A friend of mine, who's been in the life insurance business for over twenty-five years, earns a very nice income each year. He enjoys many side benefits of his success—nice things, recognition in the top five of his whole company, trips, association with other top professionals at M.D.R.T. and C.L.U. meetings. He keeps his own schedule—comes and goes when he wants.

But it wasn't always this way. His first five years were very difficult. He struggled to just barely survive. But inside him, from the very beginning, an unseen and unspoken thing had happened. He made a *commitment* to stay in the business!

He made a commitment! He obviously meant it!

In these twenty-five years, he's seen over 90 percent of the people that his company hired bomb out. They didn't stick. Most of them were just as intelligent as he. On the average, his past successes probably wouldn't have overshadowed theirs.

They set goals and made verbal commitments at the end of their sales school very much the same as he did. Most of them had no more debts or mountains to climb than my friend did. But 90 percent of them cratered while he stuck it out! Why? Why did 90 percent flake out and 10 percent stay?

I don't pretend to know all the reasons, but I do know one! Commitment!

Commitment! A few said and meant, "This is the way I'm going to spend my life, rendering service to people and receiving rewards accordingly!"

And they meant it! They stuck! Not because they had it easy or encountered fewer roadblocks than anyone else. They stayed despite roadblocks! They kept on going!

They made a *commitment!*

Now, what I'm going to say may sound pontifical, but it's a bedrock truth! Unless you make a long-term commitment to the field you're in, or the company you're with, and then grit your teeth and hang in there when the going gets tough, you're not going to enjoy the rewards and self-fulfillment you could otherwise enjoy!

Unless you make a definite commitment, there'll always be greener pastures across the road. When you've truly made a commitment, then the things I'll share in this chapter will help you build lasting success.

BE WILLING TO DO THE THING YOU FEAR!

He was a very wise man who said, "Do the thing you fear, and the death of fear is certain!" Most salespeople have come to the fork in the road, many times, where one road sign reads, "Hang in there; meet your fears head-on." The other road sign reads, "Take the easy way out. If the heat gets too great, leave the kitchen."

Yes, almost all salespeople reach this crossroad and make decisions about which road they'll take. Actually, we reach this point over and over.

In this chapter, I'll give you several strategies for dealing with fear in selling. Frankly, none of them will help unless you're willing to commit to "doing the thing you fear." It all boils down to how much you *want* to. How much *desire* you have.

What I'm telling you is the plain, unvarnished truth! You must be willing to do the thing you fear! Go where you're afraid to go. Ask when you're afraid to ask. Keep on when you want to quit.

INTEGRITY BREEDS COURAGE

A salesman once sold a car to me. He said it had no miles on it. The speedometer verified it. I found out later the car had been a demonstrator, and the speedometer had been rolled back.

The salesman made a few dollars commission on the sale. I never bought another car from him or his firm. I never referred friends to them, either. So his dishonesty made him a few dollars, but it cost him much more in repeat and referral business.

The few times I saw the salesman after that, he tried to ignore me. He didn't have the confidence to look me in my eyes. The last I heard of him, he had a crummy, little car lot—selling junky cars in a section of town populated mostly by winos and derelicts.

A friend and I were making some church visits one evening. He told me about a man named Ernie Winton who'd sold him his last car—an Oldsmobile.

"He's always calling me," my friend explained, "and asking if I'm happy with the car or having any problems. A time or two I've had minor annoyances. Ernie was like a 'hawk on a June bug!' In no time he'd be by, pick up the car, and get it fixed."

It just so happened that I was in the market for a car. Guess whom I went by to see? You got it! Ernie! He sold me a Cadillac. I didn't shop around or hassle with him. He gave me what I thought was a good deal. He didn't insult my intelligence by playing me against his salesmanager in a "turkey-plucking" negotiation.

Then for the next two years, every time a service was due, he'd call me, come by, leave his demonstrator, get mine serviced, and return it to me.

I told many people about Ernie, just as my friend had told me. I'm sure he benefited from it. I didn't buy my next car from him. I had the "hots" for another Mercedes. But when I see Ernie, he can hold his head up and not be afraid to look me in my eyeballs. He knows he served me well and that I respect him.

His integrity breeds courage!

Enduring success in almost any field of selling is not achieved by making one-shot scores, or by fleecing customers, or by outsmarting them. It's gained by repeat business, by referrals, by earning a reputation as a straight shooter.

Integrity breeds confidence!

BELIEVE IN WHAT YOU'RE SELLING

Another vital confidence-builder and fear-reducer is to honestly believe in what you're selling. Have pride in your product or service.

Several years ago, a man was in my office who was just starting a direct-marketing company. He was a cocky, arrogant, self-assured person whom it took very little effort to learn to detest.

He explained his marketing plan and gloated over the fact that he could invest under 10¢ in a product that sold for over $5.

"How do your products compare with others on the market?" I asked him.

He replied, "Oh, we don't claim to have the best products on the market; we've got the best marketing plan."

Then he tossed off my question with, "You don't have to have the best products to make the most money!"

His company flourished for a year or so. He enjoyed instant wealth and recognition. But it wasn't long before he and his organization nose-dived. He was tossed out and spent the next decade defending himself against lawsuits.

One of my good friends is a man named Robert Hunter who lives in Memphis, Tennessee. Rob worked for an all-black life insurance company for several years. Someone got him taking Shaklee food supplements. Not only did he feel better, but he especially liked the business philosophy of that organization.

He quit his job and began full-time as an independent salesperson with Shaklee. A real missionary, he sincerely wanted to help people. He does help people. He's built a fine business on this philosophy of integrity.

He believes in what he's selling. I've never known a more humble, sincere person than Rob Hunter.

His honest, deeply felt belief in what he's selling releases tremendous energy within him. He can't wait to get up and get going each morning. He'll drive for hundreds of miles to help a friend who's struggling. He takes his products personally, faithfully.

He's not out for short-range, quick scores. He's wise enough to understand that enduring success is built on rendering value and building people up.

He believes in what he's selling! This gives him confidence and reduces fear!

SEE YOURSELF AS A VALUE GENERATOR

The more that you honestly see yourself as a value generator, the more professional you'll become; and the less fear you'll have in approaching people.

What do I mean by "a value generator?" You're a value generator whenever you:

1. Sell something to someone that's more valuable to them than their money was.

2. Help people *emotionally* feel more valued than before you interacted with them.

If you sell automobiles that people enjoy more than they'd enjoy the money they paid for them, you've added value to their lives.

If you sell computer software that saves a corporate client six times as much as the service costs, you've added value to his or her company.

If you sell a YMCA membership to a person who firms up, feels better, looks better, and probably will live longer, you've added value to his or her life.

If you sell a home to a family that provides a place for them to enjoy activities, entertain friends, and take pride of ownership in; then you've added value to their lives.

Have you ever stopped and written down all the ways that *you* add value to people or companies? Why not stop right now and do that? Jot it in the margins of this book or on a note pad. Then review it daily.

How can you help people with whom you interact feel more valued? How can you build their self-esteem? How can you help fill their emotional needs?

PEOPLE REJECT YOUR OFFERING;
THEY DON'T REJECT YOU!

Well, we've thought about commitment, integrity, belief in what you're selling, and seeing yourself as a value generator. I've shown how these qualities produce real confidence and courage.

Now, let's get a bit more specific. Remember...we're talking about how to deal with fear.

Usually, when we have call-reluctance or fear of rejection, it's because *we feel* that people are *rejecting us* instead of *rejecting our products or services.* Stop and let this thought soak in for a few minutes! Look at the words I've emphasized.

It's true, isn't it?

Here, let me say that it's quite normal for you to experience pain when someone threatens or rejects you as a person. Why? Because your self-value, self-identity, or personal worth is spiritually and emotionally vital to you. When attacked, you want to fight to preserve it. But it's here that you can get confused. The confusion comes when you interpret rejection of your offering as a rejection of you personally.

Here's a little role-playing game we play in seminars I conduct. In small groups of six to eight, we have everyone look at one group member and yell with "raging emotion" these words, "No, I don't want to buy what you're selling!"

Then we have the person who receives the "abuse" calmly smile, pause, and reply, "Thank You! I know that you're rejecting my offering and not rejecting me personally! Knowing this I can still like myself and value you also!"

Sure, it's just a game, but it symbolizes the problem and the solution:

1. The problem comes when you interpret rejection of your offering as rejection of yourself.
2. The solution is to realize the difference.

When you get a "no" from a prospect, say these words to yourself slowly, "I know that you're rejecting my offering and not rejecting me personally! Knowing this, I can still like myself and value you also!"

In addition, say this over and over to yourself fifty times in the morning and fifty times in the evening. Then after three or four weeks of doing this, you'll slowly begin to mentally separate rejection of yourself from rejection of your offering.

Once programmed, your subconscious will auto-suggest this thought to you when you need it. Then you'll begin to deal with rejection more confidently.

HOW TO SET UP YOUR OWN
SUCCESS-SUPPORT SYSTEM

In the next few pages, I'm going to share with you an idea that, if it's all you learn from this book, will be worth wheelbarrow-loads of paychecks for you.

The idea I'll share with you will set up a power-generating station for you to plug into and enjoy increased strength, effectiveness, and confidence.

This concept sets in motion a natural law that empowers all who obey it. It's a force that many wealthy people have used and credit for much of their achievement. What is this natural law? This power? This force? To explain it, let me mention a word. The word is *synergism*.

Webster's New World Dictionary defines *synergism* as: "the simultaneous action of separate agencies which, together, have greater total effect than the sum of their individual effects."

What this means is that when two or more forces work together in a spirit of unity and harmony, there arises a power that's much greater than the sum of the individual parts.

Let me give you a couple of examples:

Supposedly, there was once a contest held to see whose draft work horse could pull the most weight. The winner pulled just over 9,000 pounds; the other horse pulled just under 9,000 pounds.

After the dust had settled and the owner got the bragging rights, someone came up with a question that sparked more interest. The question was, "Wonder how much both horses could pull together?"

Interest was kindled. They hooked up both horses and when they'd pulled all they could, jointly they pulled not 18,000 pounds... but over 30,000 pounds!

That's synergism! $9 + 9 = 30$!

I'm told that the C-1 missile is composed of eight Redstone rockets. But the measured thrust of a C-1 missile is twenty-four times the thrust of one Redstone rocket!

That's synergism! $8 \times 1 = 24$.

Also, I read that in the Death Valley days twenty mule-train borax workers found that it took twelve mules to pull one load of borax. However, if they added eight more mules, they could pull two loads plus a water wagon.

That's synergism! When several forces work together in a spirit of unity and harmony, there arises a power that's much greater than the sum of the individual powers!

"What does all this mean to me?" you ask. "How can it help me have more confidence and diminish fear?"

You'll soon see!

But before I tell you, let me give you another example.

In his autobiography, Benjamin Franklin explains his success. He tells that the single, most important factor in it was his involvement in a study group that met each Friday evening for mutual learning.

They met together, shared ideas they'd read, experiences they'd had, and insights they'd learned. There was mutual sharing and reinforcement of each other.

Franklin tells that, with the exception of one man who was negative and contentious and whom they kicked out of their group, the study group stayed together for over forty years.

Then he tells, one by one, what outstanding success the men achieved in their lifetimes. He gave the study group credit for generating the power for them to plug into. Franklin didn't know the word "synergism," but he well understood the power.

Well, let's get down to brass tacks! Let's get more specific. Let's talk about how you can structure your own support system—how you then can draw power from it to help you have more courage and confidence.

In cookbook fashion, let me list how to go about setting one up. Read this three or four times to get the full picture:

1. Choose two potential support-system members.
2. Qualify them:
   a. Do they share your career interests?
   b. Can you trust them to keep confidences?
   c. Are they positive and success-minded?
   d. Are they sharing, giving people?
   e. Does your emotional chemistry mix well?
   f. Will they see benefits to an association like this?
3. Visit with them:
   a. Explain the support-system concept and purpose.

      b. Tell how it'll help them enjoy greater success and confidence.

      c. Ask for commitment.

4.   What to do during your weekly meetings:

      a. Keep everything positive.

      b. Everyone shares something good that happened to her or him last week.

      c. Everyone shares something she/he has learned—a book she/he's read, an idea she/he's heard, or an experience that taught her/him something.

      d. Chairperson suggests a book, chapter, or tape message to read or listen to all this next week—points out an idea to practice.

      e. Conclude by reinforcing and building up each person.

5.   Suggestions that will help make your weekly support groups more effective:

      a. Meet for one hour at lunch or breakfast.

      b. Never argue, debate, or let negative conversation develop—it'll kill the effectiveness of your group.

      c. Don't just talk about cliché-level things—weather, sports, etc.

      d. Rotate chairperson role.

      e. Everyone agrees to keeping things confidential.

      f. Don't criticize or talk negatively about others in your meetings.

      g. Occasionally enlist the group's help in helping someone who has a need.

      h. Have one person assume the responsibility for keeping the group together and functioning.

Read and reread these instructions. Follow them to the letter. If you'll make sure the following factors are present, you'll build a dynamo from which everyone can draw power and strength:

1. Conduct meetings in a positive, noncritical, supportive environment.

2. Assign specific books, articles, or tapes that everyone reads or listens to—and practices specific points during the week.

3. Keep group talking about *application* and *practice* during meetings—not just about ideas, opinions, or intellectual concepts.

4. Give plenty of positive reinforcement—model an accepting, building attitude so each member will mirror your actions.

A success support system may be the single, most powerful thing you can do to overcome fear and build more deep-down confidence.

It plugs you into a power that defies description. It often touches spiritual forces within us.

NONJUDGMENTAL RELATIONSHIPS HELP DEVELOP COURAGE

My telephone rang one day. On the other end of the line was a man whom I'd never met, but who had graduated from one of my leadership courses.

After telling me his name, he said, "Your course has made an extra $150,000 for me in the last two years!"

That got my attention!

He went on to tell me that because of some defeats and emotional blows that he'd quit his job as an insurance salesman. Because of fear, he spent most of his days lying in bed in a fetal position.

For months, he was emotionally paralyzed. Then he enrolled in one of my nine-week leadership-training courses.

There, he was accepted and reinforced by a trained instructor. He learned that he could open up, reveal his true self, and still be accepted by the other class members.

He discovered that other people had fears also. He was inspired to take hold of his better self—to take positive action that would win over his fears.

At the end of nine weeks, he set a goal to be in the top few producers in his insurance company. He was applauded and encouraged.

Within two years, he was the number-two agent in his entire company.

What changed him?

Well, several things. But probably the most important factor was the group acceptance, support, empathy, and encouragement he found in the class.

Psychologically, we know that in order for a person to function creatively and cope with fear, disappointment, discouragement, and defeat he or she needs the support of nonjudgmental relationships.

To be emotionally healthy, we need to love and be loved. We *need* to accept and want the best to happen to others—some in a very intimate way, others, less intimately. We also *need* to have significant others in our lives who accept us and want the best to happen to us.

Here are four vital levels of relationships we need in order to function with optimum courage and minimum emotional clutter. Carefully think of these:

Level 1— A very intimate, nonjudgmental relationship with one person with whom we can be totally open and feel totally accepted. A relationship in which we feel no need to wear masks.

Level 2— An intimate, nonjudgmental relationship with two or three people wherein each and all together can give and receive unconditional support. This can be with miscellaneous friends or people with whom you work. It can also be you, your spouse, and another couple. Like level-one relationships, this one offers total acceptance of each other. In both level one and level-two relationships, people accept each other for their value as persons. Acceptance is not based on actions.

Level 3— A friendly relationship with eight to twelve people; a study group, a sales group, or other meetings of people of common interest. This group can have meaningful interaction, though less intense or intimate.

Level 4— Belonging to a larger group wherein you receive less intense support or fellowship. This can be civic clubs, luncheon groups, professional associations, churches, or other larger groups that give you enjoyment and a sense of belonging and in which you have many acquaintances.

WHAT'S ALL THIS GOT TO DO WITH SELLING?

"What's all this got to do with selling?" you ask. Everything!

You see, the relationships I've discussed influence your deep-down values, emotional feelings of worth, and spiritual concepts.

Selling is emotional! Sustained confidence in selling has to do with values and emotions. Your self-esteem—your sustained feelings of value—impacts upon your success and confidence in powerful ways.

Your integrity depends on how you see yourself. Your courage depends on how you see yourself and how you think others see you, and how much value you think you give to the lives of others! And, as I've mentioned, these impact upon spiritual forces within us.

They also get close to the root cause of fear—our self-esteem, our values, our commitment to integrity!

"PERFECT LOVE CASTS OUT FEAR!"

In the Scriptures the Apostle John writes, "There is no fear in love. Perfect love casts out fear!" The context in which he uses the word "love" is that it "seeks the highest good for others." To love is to want the best to happen to someone. What does this mean to you and me? What does it have to do with success in selling?

Hang on, I'm going to tell you!

The truth is that the more you want the best to happen to your customers, clients, or prospects...the more confidence and the less fear you'll have!

When you have this attitude, you bring powerful spiritual forces to your aid. You lose some of your fear of rejection. You become other-centered, not self-centered. You appear more professional to your clients. You persuade with the highest form of persuasion—integrity! You instill trust and confidence.

You play in a different league!

SUMMING UP

Well, I hope what I've said in this chapter challenges you. It's not what you've read in most sales books. But I believe that integrity is the basic cause of sustained high-performance selling, of real, 24-karat professional selling.

I've thrown far too much at you in this chapter for you to internalize in just a few readings. So I hope you'll come back and re-read it several dozen times.

Read Emerson's essay on "Compensation" to better understand the true cause-and-effect of selling success. Read Napoleon Hill's books—*Think and Grow Rich, The Law of Success,* and *The Master Key to Riches*—especially the chapters on the Master-Mind concept. You'll better understand the psychology behind a success support system.

I want to leave you with the thought that selling isn't learning and doing a bag of tricks. It isn't outsmarting people, cutting them off at the pass, or conning them.

Everything in life is cause and effect. For every effect, there's been a consistent cause. Every cause produces a like effect. This is a law that can't be long violated.

Now, let me say that what I've given you in the chapters of this book, if practiced, is enough for you to significantly increase your sales, lifestyle, income, professionalism, and self-value.

Throughout this book, I've tried to present the ideas to you with honesty, realism, and blood-and-guts emotion. Like selling really is.

Frankly, I must tell you that if you only *read* this book, you'll have wasted your time! But if you'll *live* with it for several months—devour it, underline, mark in margins, assimilate, and apply the principles, you'll benefit greatly.

I hope you'll spend time with this book daily for the next several months.

Practice until you've developed the six-step system and other strategies into strong habits.

Commit to doing the things you fear. Go where you're afraid to go. See people you're afraid to see. Ask when you're afraid to ask.

Commit and persist. Work through the pain. You'll emerge a strong, seasoned, wise, and wealthy person.

Commitment and persistence are the price you must pay!

Thank you for spending your time and money on this book. For allowing our lives to mix. For enriching my life by allowing me to be part of your support mechanism.

Afterword

The great mind of Emerson, in his essay on "Self-Reliance," expressed this lofty thought:

> "The voyage of the best ship is a zigzag line of a hundred tacks. See the line from a sufficient distance, and it straightens itself to the average tendency."

My good friend, your selling will follow the same course: zigzags, ups and downs, high points, low points, successes and disappointments.

Every successful person's life follows this pattern!

But as we examine others' successes from afar, we tend only to see the upward curve. We rarely see the hidden agonies that were suffered in the struggle.

I say this so you'll understand your ups and downs: so you'll see that you're normal, so you won't lose heart; so discouragement won't victimize you, and so you won't quit!

When times get tough, keep sailing! When you get so many rejections you want to cover your head and surrender, keep sailing!

When you don't know how you're going to eat or pay your bills tomorrow, keep sailing! When adverse winds seem surely to break you, keep sailing!

For as surely as you do, you'll pull through victoriously!

And one day, you'll learn that every salesperson of achievement fought the same battles and uncertainties that you thought were uniquely yours!

Sail on, my friend, sail on!

And, good selling!

Willingham's Wisdom

There was once a caring sales trainer named Willingham,
Who in this book has put all the ideas he could cram.
  It's with intense love and affection,
  That he gives you this direction,
With the hope that your success explodes with a Bam!

Index

INDEX

INDEX